Cultural
WhiplaSh

OTHER BOOKS BY PATRICK GARRY

An American Paradox
Censorship in a Nation of Free Speech

The American Vision of a Free Press
*An Historical and Constitutional Revisionist View
of the Press as a Marketplace of Ideas*

Liberalism and American Identity

A Nation of Adversaries
How the Litigation Explosion Is Reshaping America

Rediscovering a Lost Freedom
The First Amendment Right to Censor Unwanted Speech

Scrambling for Protection
The New Media and the First Amendment

Wrestling with God
The Courts' Tortuous Treatment of Religion

Cultural WhiρlaSh

THE UNFORESEEN CONSEQUENCES OF AMERICA'S CRUSADE AGAINST RACIAL DISCRIMINATION

Patrick Garry

CUMBERLAND HOUSE
NASHVILLE, TENNESSEE

CULTURAL WHIPLASH
PUBLISHED BY CUMBERLAND HOUSE PUBLISHING, INC.
431 Harding Industrial Drive
Nashville, Tennessee 37211

Cover design by Gore Studio, Inc., Nashville, Tennessee

Library of Congress Cataloging-in-Publication Data
Garry, Patrick M.
  Cultural whiplash : the unforeseen consequences of America's crusade against racial discrimination / Patrick Garry.
     p. cm.
  Includes bibliographical references and index.
  ISBN-13: 978-1-58182-569-5 (hardcover : alk. paper)
  ISBN-10: 1-58182-569-2 (hardcover : alk. paper)
  1. Racism—United States. 2. United States—Race relations. 3. United States—Social conditions. I. Title.
E184.A1G19 2006
305.800973—dc22   2006024377

Printed in the United States of America
1 2 3 4 5 6 7 8 9 10—10 09 08 07 06

For Michael and Elizabeth

ContenTs

IntroductiOn

DURING THE CIVIL RIGHTS movement of the 1960s, the crusade against racism was one of social justice and moral necessity. Forty years later, however, the issue of racial discrimination is surrounded by fear, guilt, and confusion.

Even as the antidiscrimination laws get stronger, even as the race studies departments in universities proliferate, even as corporate diversity training courses multiply, even as affirmative action programs become institutionalized, racial discrimination is claimed to be as pervasive as ever. African Americans are succeeding as never before, yet even the most successful still claim to be victimized by persistent racism. Arrests of young black males are said to be motivated by racism, even when the arresting police officer is black. Teachers are portrayed as racists when they discipline black students, but they are also portrayed as racists if they allow black students to be measured under a more lenient standard. Indeed, accusations of racism know no bounds. The federal government's sluggish response to Hurricane Katrina was alleged to have been racist simply because many of the people affected were black.

The clarity of the civil rights movement during the 1960s resulted in large part from its moral character. Ending racial discrimination was part of a larger quest to achieve a more moral and just society. Thus, moral values were an intricate element in the pursuit of civil rights. But such is not the case now. The antidiscrimination crusade has become driven by a warped sense of equality, which in turn has been used to erode the moral foundation of society. Any moral judgment or cultural value that criticizes certain types of social behavior—for example, sexual promiscuity, dishonesty, unethical conduct, or defiance of authority—is seen as violating the rule against discrimination. Consequently, instead of elevating the moral character of society, the antidiscrimination mind-set pushes behavioral standards to the lowest common denominator.

Even though race has become the defining cultural morality issue, it has simultaneously prompted a moral retreat within society. This retreat has resulted from the increasing uncertainty surrounding "subconscious" racism—a racism of which the racist is unaware because it has become so camouflaged it cannot be detected by the unassisted eye. Under such an ambiguous definition, almost any action that might ultimately affect a racial minority in a negative way can be depicted as racist. Consequently, individuals do not know when or how they might be accused of racism. They refrain from voicing opinions not only on racial matters but on any other moral issue that might somehow possess a racial dimension. Yet when racial minorities are relieved of moral duties, it is but a short step to relieve the larger culture of those same duties. In a society committed to equality, a two-tiered system of moral values cannot exist for long.

The real danger posed by the current racial climate in America is not that the races will ultimately fail to live together in harmony; the real danger goes far beyond the matter of race relations—it goes to the moral identity of society as a whole. The danger is that the current climate of racial politics will contribute to a moral gutting of society, leaving it without the one trait necessary for the final and complete eradication of racism.

In principle, a democratic society should turn a blind eye to the race, color, creed, and gender of its citizens. This color-blind approach adopted by Martin Luther King Jr. provided a unifying energy to the civil rights movement. It not only gave voice to racial minorities seeking social justice, it also inspired the larger culture to mobilize against racism. Because of its clarity and evenhandedness, the color-blind ideal served an important educational role: it revealed the inherent wrong of racism while at the same time showing the path toward rehabilitation.

Currently, however, the color-blind approach is said to be just another aspect of racism. It is said to be the rock behind which racists hide when opposing policies such as racial preferences. And yet, as the approach continues to fall from favor during this present era of affirmative action, racial divisions in society continue to deepen, with racial segregation intensifying and racial confusion spreading.

There is absolutely no doubt that the civil rights movement achieved a heroic and vital goal in America. Nor is there any doubt as to the moral depravity of racism. But as America has discovered a half century after its modern civil rights crusade began, antidiscrimination charges can have a backlash effect. Even if initially motivated by the good intentions of achieving social justice, they can boomerang against those intentions and turn against society. Hence, they are not cost-free; they can no longer be asserted without any concern for the negative side effects they might impose on America's moral and cultural values.

The steady stream of charges of racism is wearing down society's confidence in its moral capacity. When society is repeatedly accused of being inherently racist, and hence inherently immoral, people lose confidence in their individual and collective ability to do good. When civil rights leaders allege that racism today is just as invidious as it was during the 1950s, society loses all faith in its capacity for moral growth. This in turn drives society into a moral emptiness, making it afraid to enforce any moral standards for fear of being tagged with discrimination.

This book examines the corrosive side effects of the modern antidiscrimination crusade. It examines how the automatic granting of moral supremacy to any argument asserted in the name of antidiscrimination has had a backlash effect on the cultural foundations of the nation.

Chapter 1 gives an overview of the confusing and morally suffocating state of racial attitudes and assumptions in contemporary America. It also outlines society's moral retreat in connection with race as well as the effect that presumptions of racism have had on the authority of social institutions.

A discussion of how racism has become so broad and ambiguous that it can be alleged in nearly unlimited situations or circumstances appears in chapter 2. Racism is now defined in a way that almost guarantees its continuing existence. Indeed, nowhere are claims of racial discrimination more common than academia, which is easily the national institution that is most embracing of racial diversity.

Because of the unlimited reach of racism and the resulting uncertainty over what constitutes racist behavior, a labyrinth of contradictions has arisen in the area of race. This maze of contradictions is surveyed in chapter 3. It is a self-perpetuating cycle: the more confusing and contradictory our racial climate becomes, the greater the fear arises from being branded a racist. But the contradictions extend well beyond black-white relations; they also permeate relations between the different racial groups increasingly populating America. In this respect, the double standards inherent in racial preference programs become unsustainable.

Chapter 4 examines how the antidiscrimination crusade fits into the rise of moral relativism and how the interaction of these two social movements has resulted in a weakening of the moral and cultural character of the nation. Ironically, a climate of moral relativism makes it increasingly difficult to achieve the moral goal of true social justice. Furthermore, because racial discrimination has come to constitute society's primary, if not exclusive, moral wrong, it can often have a crowding-out effect on all other moral or ethical concerns, as if "racial correctness" is the only true measure of moral or ethical character. For instance, the same corporations that spend billions on diversity sensitivity programs spend almost nothing on business ethics training, but this contradicts Martin Luther King Jr.'s hope of using racial justice to elevate the overall moral character of society.

The moral erosion caused by the current racial mind-set is discussed in chapter 5. This erosion begins when society, fearful of charges of racism, refrains from judging or criticizing the destructive social behavior of its racial minorities. But because of the constant influence of the equality principle, this tolerance must then extend back to the majority. Thus, to avoid even the possibility of allegations of racism, many institutions such as schools and law-enforcement agencies are lowering their standards not just for minorities but for all Americans. Consequently, the most antisocial behavior of the most marginalized members of the underclass becomes the behavioral model for mainstream society. This is a model that blames high incarceration rates not on criminal behavior but on overly harsh laws.

The political forces that have created and perpetuated this perverse climate of racial dictates and sensitivities are analyzed in chapter 6. This chapter also reveals how the forces most visibly opposed to racism are the ones most committed to making sure that racism never disappears from America. In a strategy aimed at solidifying a "race coalition," these forces have tried to equate opposing political philosophies with racism, as exemplified by the often virulent white liberal attack on black conservatives. By smearing conservatism with the stain of racism, white liberals can accuse black conservatives of being indifferent or oppressive to racial minorities. This use of racial politics, however, has been used to do more than just attack conservatives; it has become a tool in a much broader crusade to transform the cultural identity of America from an assimilated society into an adversarial culture composed of fragmented ethnic and racial groups.

Chapter 7 explores the use of race as a tool in a much larger cultural revolution. Because of the power of race, and because of the unquestioned social abhorrence of racism, it has been used to attack an array of cultural values and institutions lying at the heart of the American experience. By using race to discredit all aspects of a society that once tolerated slavery, cultural revolutionaries can then undermine the legitimacy of Western civilization as a whole. And this attack on the cultural core of America has made the nation uncertain, defensive, and apologetic about everything from illegal immigration to foreign policy.

The role of white guilt in contributing to the perverse racial climate in America today is examined in chapter 8. This guilt has not only prompted a retreat from many of the essential moral questions surrounding race, but it has inspired social policies that in fact do further harm to African Americans. In this respect, it resembles the kind of cultural appeasement that has proved so damaging in Europe with respect to its Muslim immigrants.

The intensifying racial conflict between Europeans and Muslim immigrants arises in large part because the nations of Europe have never expected or even encouraged immigrants to conform with basic Western cultural norms. For instance, when the Danes introduced some controls against forced marriage, they were accused of racism. Seeking not to offend Muslims, Norwegian social and cultural workers refrain from criticizing the slavery and female genital mutilation practiced in some Islamic countries. In Holland, teachers are reluctant to teach about World War II in schools attended by Muslim students, because those students refuse to accept the reality of the Holocaust. A school director, hoping to avoid offending Muslim pupils, advised native students in February 2005 to remove the little Dutch flags they had sewn onto their school bags. In doing so, the director essentially took for granted that the Muslim children were profoundly anti-Dutch.

This same type of withdrawal, retreat, and appeasement is occurring in America, though not nearly to the extremes that it is in Europe. And it is occurring not because of any rational decision but because of how the antidiscrimination crusade has been diverted from its original path.

Cultural WhiplaSh

ONE

=============

In the Wake
of the
AntiDiscrimination
CruSade

THEY WERE eleventh graders; they never sat still for anything. But on this particular day, they sat very still, very compliantly, nodding their heads every few seconds.

The guest speaker was in his midtwenties. He paced back and forth across the front of the room as he spoke. His speech flowed as steady as water from a faucet. He was obviously accustomed to speaking to all-white audiences.

"The thing about racism is that it's like this invisible virus. It's everywhere—and it has completely infected the white gene. . . ."

The students in the front row nodded the most eagerly. But no one looked around; no one glanced at anyone else—they kept their eyes glued on the speaker.

"It's there all right, but nobody admits to it. Take this school, for instance. No one will admit to any racism going on, but just look around—how many black faces do you see? And your parents—sure, maybe they watch *Oprah* or follow Tiger, but why do you think they put you in this lily-white school? You think racism's not involved? . . ."

The nods were a little more squeamish, but they still came.

"Don't think you're immune, 'cause you're not. The only question is whether you're gonna have guts enough to admit it. . . ."

This time, accompanying the nods, were faces with tightened foreheads that had become furrowed, eyes that had narrowed.

Inviting this speaker had been the teacher's idea. He was passionate about the cause; he had participated in civil rights marches during the late 1960s. In addition to this course, he taught a class on race in America. Many times before he had told his students the same things this guest speaker was saying now, but the teacher knew the words needed a face to go with them.

After the speaker had finished and left the room, ten minutes remained in the class period. The teacher asked if there were any questions.

"Why are there no black teachers here?" a student barked out.

"Why don't you admit more minority students?"

"How can you work at such a racist institution?"

"You always talk about the 1960s, but why don't you do something now? Why do all the teachers just sit by and let the racism continue?"

The questions didn't go exactly as the teacher had expected. And for the first time, he felt a little embarrassed about the large poster of Martin Luther King that hung on the wall.

Later, when he walked with the class to the cafeteria, he felt even more self-conscious as they passed one of the ninth-grade classrooms, the outside of which was decorated with student drawings on the theme of racial healing.

• • •

Perhaps that evening there were dinner conversations that mirrored the one between Lisa, one of the eleventh graders, and her parents.

"Your friends always talk about racism, but how come you live in a neighborhood that's all white?" Lisa asked.

"We didn't move here because it was all white."

"That doesn't really answer the question. I mean, the point is, it's all white. If you really wanted to do something about racism, why don't you get black people to move here? Or why don't we move? This place makes me sick sometimes. That school makes me sick sometimes."

"Sweetheart, did something . . . ?"

"All those prissy white moms always driving up to the school in their SUVs—it just makes me sick."

"Are you saying we're racist? Is that what you're saying?"

"Did something happen at school today?"

"Lisa, if someone at that school is accusing us of racism, I want to know."

"What are you going to do, Daddy? Give me another lecture about what a political saint you were in college? You and my teacher, you're both the same. You send me to schools where I read poetry by Maya Angelou and study African history, but what difference does it make? It's still all racist. Your generation got a few laws passed, big deal. You just . . . you have no idea . . ."

He sat in stunned silence as his daughter stomped out of the room. He had always taken pride in how he had raised her. It was one of the few things he had done right, one of the few things on which he had done better than his own parents.

RACE IN America is described as the elephant in the room that no one wants to talk about. During the Bill Clinton presidency, Hillary Rodham Clinton suggested a "national conversation" on race as if it were a subject never discussed or even acknowledged. But in the year 2003 alone, according to WorldCat, 776 books were published on the subject of racism, and almost 8,000 newspaper articles addressed racial issues. Entire genres of popular music, like hip-hop and rap, focus on race, and in 2003 nearly one hundred million copies of hip-hop and rap CDs were sold.

The problem is not silence but confusion, at least as far as many nonminorities are concerned. During the civil rights era of the 1960s, racial discrimination was easy to spot. It resided in laws that made it more difficult for minorities to vote and laws that sanctioned segregation in schools. It was found in employers' refusal to hire black workers. It could be seen in a university's denial of admission to minority students. During the 1960s, it was easy for whites to join the crusade against racism. The enemy was clear, the remedy obvious. But now everything is different. Now we are in a time of subtle, subconscious, or invisible racism. But by moving into the realm of the subconscious, race has stepped beyond the bounds of objective definition, pushing nonminorities ever deeper into racial confusion.

A group of older alumni of a Maryland high school decided to hold a reunion for those who graduated during the 1940s and 1950s. But since segregation was practiced then, and the school was not desegregated until 1969, the reunion involved only white alumni. This all-white reunion, according to civil rights activists, amounted to racism.[1]

Teachers and parents at a San Francisco school attended mostly by immigrant children from thirty-one different countries opposed a city plan to move another school into its crowded building.[2] They argued that class sizes were already too large, making it difficult for the students to learn English. But their opposition was labeled as racist, because the other school seeking to move in served primarily black and Latino students.

The Chicago City Colleges' board of trustees sued a teachers' union for publishing a column critical of affirmative action in its newsletter.[3] Free speech was not the issue, said the board, which characterized the column as illegal racial harassment.

A university professor assigned Mark Twain's *Huckleberry Finn* to his class. Offended by both the racial language in the novel and the heated class discussions about race relations, a student filed a racial harassment claim with the university.[4] Another student filed a similar complaint when a law professor at the George Mason University School of Law chose to discuss verbal torts by using a hypothetical case involving a Ku Klux Klan march through a black community. The student alleged the ensuing discussion subjected her to a racially hostile environment.[5]

Even though elite universities such as Harvard are admitting more and more black students, African American educators are still critical. The reason is because the black students are not the "right kind" of black students.[6] As children of recent West Indian and African immigrants, these students are not the ones for whom affirmative action admissions policies were primarily intended—namely, the descendants of American slaves.

It is argued that standardized tests are racist, but how can mathematical equations be racist? It is argued that racism is unique to whites, but what explains the statement made in *Washington Post* reporter Nathan McCall's book, *Makes Me Wanna Holler,* that even as a professional journalist he still had the urge to "take one of those white boys where I work and bang his head against a wall or stomp him in the ground until all the stress leaves my body." School curricula are supposedly biased against racial minorities, but why do more schoolchildren know about Martin Luther King Jr. than they do about James Madison?

All these racial nuances are confusing to nonminorities. To civil rights activists, however, the situation is relatively simple: racial prejudice is at the root of everything. Every negative cultural condition or economic statistic flows from racial attitudes. The high black population in the nation's prisons is the result of a racist criminal justice system. The higher unemployment rates of blacks are due to an economy pervaded by racism. When a black teenager is arrested, it is because of his race. If a black business owner is refused a loan, it's because of her race. If a black employee is denied a promotion, it's because of his race. And yet as more racial accusations are levied, society becomes more divided, more wounded, and more incapable of healing itself. It is like a prosecutor who never stops accusing and indicting, never allowing a chance for the jury to issue its resolving verdict.

No one can make the claim that racism has been completely eliminated, but it is equally outrageous to deny that substantial progress has been made. The black middle class has never been larger. The percentage of black households earning in excess of fifty thousand dollars a year more than doubled from 1971 to 2001.[7] More blacks own homes than at any time in the past.[8] There are more blacks in college and more black college graduates than ever before. Within the Bush administration, a record number of blacks have held high-level governmental posts. These gains and accomplishments, however, are frequently ignored. Colin Powell, the first black secretary of state, was dismissed as just a "token." Some even saw Powell as further evidence of the pervasive yet subtle racism in society—a racism that seeks to camouflage itself by elevating a few chosen minorities to high-visibility positions.

The continuing allegations of "subtle racism" leave the majority in a no-win situation. Whenever a racial minority is statistically underrepresented, racism can be blamed. But whenever that minority makes progress, it can be passed off as mere tokenism. Consequently, the more gains made by minorities, the more confusing the racial situation seems to become and the more contradictory the allegations of racism.

Actor Denzel Washington talks about the immense difficulties of life as an African American, and Danny Glover describes America as a racist country. Director Spike Lee complains of being victimized by the white establishment. Richard Williams, father of tennis stars Venus and Serena Williams, says that "black people [in America] don't really have an opportunity at nothin'."[9] Yet all these men have experienced success beyond the wildest dreams of the vast majority of white Americans; their incomes exceed those of 99 percent of all Americans.

If racism is pervasive, if it controls the lives and fates of all African Americans, then why have some blacks prospered tremendously while others have languished in crime and poverty? If black men and black women are equally exposed to social racism, why does the economic performance of black women mirror that of white women?

It is argued that black motorists are stopped more frequently by highway patrol officers, but how can an officer tell the racial identity of the driver of a car several hundred yards away, and at night? Poor academic performance of black students is blamed on racism in the schools, and yet black students are accused by other blacks of "acting white" if they try too hard in school. The underrepresentation of blacks in the fields of engineering and accounting is seen as evidence of racism, and yet the overrepresentation of blacks in the fields of sports and entertainment is given no racial significance. In affirmative action cases involving universities, racial diversity is said to be vital to the educational process, and yet this argument is rarely made with respect to all-black colleges. When the University of Georgia in March 2004 decided to consider race in its admissions process, the *Atlanta Journal-Constitution* praised the decision as sound education policy. "Diversity holds rewards for all students," the editors wrote,[10] even though just a mile away from the *Journal-Constitution* offices are two virtually all-black colleges.

Contrary to the claims of civil rights activists, maybe everything isn't "all about race." Maybe it's all about politics. Maybe, underlying everything, politics is at the heart of the conflict. This possibility is reflected in the bitter clash between mainstream African American civil rights leaders and conservative blacks. Advocating a distinctly minority position within their racial group, conservative blacks have been slandered as "ventriloquists' dummies" and "black hustlers" and "racial Benedict Arnolds." But if such bitter divisions can occur even within the same racial group, then perhaps race is not the determinant of all our social conflicts—maybe politics is.

St. John's Lutheran Church was in the heart of the city, just two miles from downtown. During the 1970s, the parish had almost disbanded, and the church was nearly torn down. But it made a comeback in the 1990s, when young professionals started moving into newly renovated condos. Kathryn joined the parish in 1991 after attending her first AA meeting in the church basement. For three years, she never missed a meeting; she went to worship services every Sunday and volunteered for as many church projects as her new job would allow. St. John's, she told everyone, had turned her life around.

One morning when she arrived for Sunday services, she encountered a protester on the church's front steps. The protester held a sign proclaiming "Racism is alive and well at St. John's." Kathryn recognized the man—he had been hired as a parish social worker. There had been rumors of problems, but this was the first Kathryn had heard of racism.

After a story appeared in the newspaper, the number of protesters grew. Kathryn didn't recognize them, but neither did she look very closely at their faces—she mostly tried to sneak in the side door. And then, one Sunday, she just stayed in bed and didn't bother going to church. She even quit the AA meetings. She hated racism and didn't want to be associated with it in any way. The minister called her a couple of times, but she never returned the calls. She was ashamed of how she handled it, but she didn't want to find herself on the side of a bunch of white supremacists. She never did learn how the dispute was resolved. She wasn't alone, though—she'd heard that lots of people had done just what she'd done.

America, rightly so, honors and celebrates the leaders of the civil rights movement. As with any crusade of social justice, those initial crusaders for civil rights were heroic and courageous. It was not easy to oppose all the social inertia that had been built up on the side of racial bigotry, but the future of America depended on it. And in time, more than a half century since *Brown v. Board of Education*, society has learned how to recognize, confront, and adjudicate accusations of racial discrimination.

The civil rights crusade was a necessary and constructive experience. In recent years, however, certain negative side effects of the antidiscrimination crusade have come to light. Charges of racism have become so widespread and pervasive, so automatically asserted, that they have done more than just correct instances of racist behavior—they have led to profound condemnations of the national culture. Society has responded much like Kathryn did in the example above: because of charges of racism, regardless of the truth, she came to doubt everything else connected to that charge. When a personnel officer is accused of racial discrimination in the handling of one applicant, a subtle indictment goes out to the entire corporation and all its employees. When a defendant alleges racial bias in the prosecution's case against him, a suspicion of racism hangs over the entire criminal justice system. When singer Michael Jackson is arrested for child abuse, he is seen as a victim of a racist society, even though that society has given him wealth and fame.

When stories of past racial bigotry and segregation are continually recounted, as if such behavior still exists today, a moral downgrading of society occurs. It is seen as pervasively racist and hence incapable of acting with any moral purpose. Of course, if society is so irreparably racist, then it deserves to have its moral authority wiped away. But if it is not, then the widespread and almost instinctive allegations of racial discrimination are inflicting a costly social injury. Their mere existence causes an erosion of trust and respect from all of society's institutions. And as these institutions lose their trust and respect, they lose their sources of moral energy.

Charges of racism have become particularly powerful because they have bucked the trend of other socially recognized "sins." Under the influence of moral relativism, society now refuses to judge many types of behavior that were once seen as being morally suspect. Promiscuity, divorce, out-of-wedlock births, casual drug use, employee "liberties" with corporate property, and "fudged" expense reports are all either quietly ignored or publicly accepted. Bill Clinton lied under oath, and the public simply decided to "move on." Jesse Jackson diverted charitable funds to support the mother of his illegitimate child, and there was hardly a public murmur. Just about any moral transgression or ethical lapse qualifies for "move on" status—except for racial matters. When it comes to racial sins, there is no moral relativism, no "moving on."

In many respects, racism has become the sole cultural sin—the only social wrong that merits universal condemnation. Hence, charges of racial discrimination have the power to completely disable the moral authority of any person or institution. If one church official is accused of a racist act, every aspect of that church's work and mission is morally discredited. Just the suspicion of the sin of racism is enough to immediately wipe away all moral virtue or identity from an individual or institution. Indeed, the danger with accusations of racism is that their mere assertion is enough to impute guilt; for when it comes to racism, the presumption is "guilty until proven innocent."

As it stands now, charges of racial discrimination travel a one-way street. They are asserted but rarely defended. And through their assertion, they can inflict damage on an area far wider than that of their specific target. In today's society, charges of racism are like a nuclear explosion—they may be aimed at a precise target, but the fallout can extend far beyond.

Afraid of being trapped in the fallout, whites have retreated into a kind of moral cocoon, afraid of doing anything that might be interpreted as racist and willing to make any moral sacrifice so as to evade the racist label. They are reluctant to set moral standards or make seemingly nonracial moral judgments, lest those judgments somehow acquire a racial edge. There is a fear of condemning the violent and sexually explicit lyrics of rap music, since many rap artists are black. (When a white student in a black-music history class at Berkeley observed that rap lyrics were misogynistic, several black students dressed her down to the point of tears.) There is a hesitancy to impose dress codes, lest those codes impact certain racial minorities. There is a reluctance to vigorously denounce gang membership, lest it be revealed that certain minorities populate certain gangs. There is even a fear of criticizing illegal immigration, since many illegal immigrants are also from racial minorities. Each year, largely out of a fear of being called racist should it act otherwise, America spends more than seven billion dollars to educate the children of illegal immigrants.[11] So while a national conversation on race sounds like a good idea, nonminorities may have little incentive to join in, because nothing muffles white Americans more than the fear of being called racist.

The uncertainty as to what acts may later lead to charges of racism has contributed to a crisis of virtue, where the majority culture shies away from taking moral stands, shrinking back into the safety of individual isolation. If racial attitudes define social virtue, then the ambiguous nature of the former will effectively torpedo the pursuit of the latter. Vice thrives on ignorance and ambiguity; virtue requires knowledge and certainty. The sinner can neither repent nor reform if she does not know the true nature of the sin. Fear and undefined guilt are conducive neither to the development of virtue nor to open and honest communication.

Mark was a passenger in Kevin's car on the foggy night that Kevin struck and killed a man walking along the road. Kevin was an all-state baseball player, but his college athletic scholarship was revoked when he pled guilty to involuntary manslaughter. After a brief stint in prison, Kevin found a job driving a cement truck—but he never found a way out of his bitterness.

They were once best friends, but now Mark and Kevin no longer speak. For years, Kevin kept finding new ways to blame Mark for the accident. Mark didn't relish encountering Kevin on the street; he never knew how or when the subject of the accident would come up, or in what way he would be blamed yet again.

Plagued with guilt over the racism of the past, whites are beset with a moral uncertainty over any racial issue. This uncertainty breeds anxiety, followed by fear, which in turn further erodes any capacity for moral rigor. During his 2004 presidential campaign, John Kerry was fearful of addressing actor Bill Cosby's comments that blacks should take more responsibility for their problems.[12]

Because of this uncertainty and fear, race is given an untouchable status, trumping every other issue. This is why the Equal Employment Opportunity Commission has supported discrimination lawsuits against a life insurance company that fired a black employee who committed expense account fraud, an oil company that fired a minority employee who stole corporate property and falsified expense reports, a company that fired a secretary for refusing to answer the telephone, and the post office for refusing to hire a mail carrier whose driver's license had been suspended four times.[13] But in a society based on egalitarianism, moral exemptions granted to one group are eventually extended across society as a whole, resulting in a lowering of cultural behavioral standards throughout society.

The grandfather started the business. In the 1950s, a new factory was built—it was the largest employer in town. But foreign competition brought cutbacks in the 1970s; at the same time, the workers joined a union and demanded a substantial pay raise. By now, his son had taken over the business. He didn't have his father's affection for the town and had spent his youth attending private schools in the East. So he dug in his heels, and when the union struck, he bused in scab workers. After he broke the union and hired back the old workers, he cut their health benefits and increased their hours.

The son retired in the late 1980s and passed the business on to his three children. They tried to make things right with the town. They built a day-care facility adjacent to the factory; they paid for the workers to take night classes; they didn't lay off anyone during the economic downturn in 1991. But the town wasn't quick to forgive. When the family began planning to install robotic welders on one of the assembly lines, the workers protested, seeing it as part of a scheme to replace them with machines. Then the mayor got involved, notifying the family that the city would raise taxes if it made any changes to the factory.

Several years later, the family announced plans to purchase another factory in the next state. Again a protest ensued. It was all part of a plan to relocate and leave the town high and dry, the mayor alleged. A group of city council members promised to go to court to prevent the purchase. The children were just like their father, the townspeople said.

A year later, the family sold the business to a multinational corporation that immediately terminated half the workforce. The siblings took the sale proceeds and left town.

If people are constantly condemned as sinners, they will eventually become sinners. A constant imputing of guilt can make even the innocent act in ways that eventually warrant that guilt. If a person is continually accused of committing undefined crimes, she will probably give up the futile attempt of trying to prove her innocence and simply end up settling for a life of crime. When there is no realistic chance of redemption, what motivates a wrongdoer to reform? If the town in the story above does not let the children shake free of the sins of their father, then they will have little choice but to become the sinner their father was. And so it is with race.

Charges of racial discrimination are useless if they do not lead to improved and enlightened race relations; they are simply ways of further dividing society. After all the decades of civil rights activism, America is more racially divided than ever before. Unless the rest of society feels that progress is being made, it will eventually dismiss the continual assertion of racism charges as mere acts of anger and vengeance. This is the dilemma faced by contemporary America. If, as civil rights activists claim, racism is as entrenched in America as it was a half century ago, then why should society even continue to participate in the racial justice process? On the other side, if minorities believe that whites are inherently incapable of racial tolerance, then why even try for integration?

The history faculty of a small state college embarked on a search for a new professor. Of the seven current members of the department, three were women and two were Asian. It was hoped that the new hire would further increase faculty diversity.

The two finalists were both women. One was white, the other African American. But serious problems arose in the research presentation given by the latter. After several meetings of heated debate, the faculty voted four to three to offer the position to the white woman. When notified of this decision, the rejected applicant threatened a racial discrimination lawsuit. In a follow-up meeting, the faculty decided that the only fair response would be to hire an outside party to investigate the faculty's racial attitudes and determine if in fact they had acted in a discriminatory manner or had been guilty of subtle racism.

Perhaps the blame for all the confusion surrounding "subtle racism" should be placed on whites. If whites are not willing to look closely and honestly into their hearts, then the question of subtle racism will never be answered. Whites cannot shirk their responsibility on this matter by simply abdicating all moral judgment to racial minorities.

During a racial-sensitivity training session at the University of Cincinnati, the facilitator singled out a woman and mocked her as "a member of the privileged white elite." The facilitator demeaned the woman's three academic degrees, saying they were a mere genetic entitlement. Later in the session, when the facilitator once again ordered the woman to stand and face more abuse, the woman just sat and sobbed. Sitting silently and submissively in their seats, not one of her approximately one hundred white colleagues rose to her defense.

In a world in which racial discrimination is the primary social sin, whites need to find a way to achieve some sense of virtue. This need for virtue is not simply a matter of self-interest. It is not simply a way to dismiss or ignore past wrongs, nor is it a way for whites to feel a naive sense of self-righteousness. The quest for virtue is one that all society, every person within society, should be rewarded for pursuing. A healthy democracy depends on citizens striving to be virtuous, and that pursuit will only occur if citizens actually believe that virtue is possible. Without such a belief, individuals will give up on virtue and slide into lifestyles of hedonistic narcissism and self-absorption.

Within the current climate of race relations, there appears to be only one way for whites to achieve virtue, and this is through politics—

the path chosen by white liberals. A support of vigorous affirmative action programs, expanded civil rights laws, and educational standards and curricula catering to the cultural backgrounds of African Americans has helped insulate white liberals from accusations of racism. In addition, a condemnation of Western culture, a repudiation of the writings of "dead white males," and a suspicious attitude toward police and the criminal justice system have also served as ideological components of white racial virtue.

The degree to which this political path toward racial virtue has succeeded can be seen in the extent to which its nonpractitioners are condemned. There is no group in society more presumed to hold racist views than white conservatives, no group more accused of racial insensitivity and of harboring a desire to return to the segregationist days of the pre-1960s. Indeed, by depicting their political opponents as racists, white liberals hope to be seen as the opposite, thus clinging to a shaky sense of racial virtue. Without a trace of hesitation or impunity, white liberals accuse Republicans of actively conspiring to deprive African Americans of the right to vote. The Florida election fiasco in 2000 was blamed on Republicans' seeking to disenfranchise black voters. In the 2004 presidential campaign, political advertisements portrayed the White House door as being closed to African Americans. The No Child Left Behind Act was depicted as a Republican ploy to recreate a segregated educational system. Clearly, the message is: if you're white and conservative, you're presumptively racist. This is particularly evident on the issue of welfare reform. Republican criticism of the welfare system has often been interpreted as a cloaked expression of racist attitudes. On the other hand, when President Clinton signed the welfare reform bill in 1996, his opposition to existing welfare programs was given no racial significance.

• • •

IN AMERICA, where racial discrimination is seen as the primary if not exclusive social sin, the crusade against discrimination is waged as if in a cultural vacuum. Consequently, accusations of racism are seen in a no-lose light—at best, they fight racism; at worst, they educate the public on the need to keep fighting racism. But as important as it is, discrimination is not the only social concern, nor are discrimination charges a cost-free endeavor. As it has evolved in America, our racial climate has contributed to an erosion of the wider cultural morality. And this result completely contradicts the message of Martin Luther King Jr., who preached that racial justice could only occur amid a heightened moral order within society as a whole.

TWO

The Fog
of
RaciSm

MICHAEL STEELE was the registrar at a small state university. He was also the only African American administrator at the institution.

Things were going badly for the registrar's office. The new computer registration system was experiencing lots of flaws, and the registrar was taking the heat.

Just days before spring registration was to begin, a notice went out from the president's office, informing students and faculty that any questions or concerns about the new computer system should be directed to the assistant register. Rumors immediately circulated that Steele had been fired, and the fact that the president's office had made no mention of Steele's sudden absence only fueled those rumors.

Thomas Honerman, an associate professor in the English department, had been having his own problems: his tenure application was receiving negative reviews. When he heard the rumors about Steele, he was outraged. He fired off a harsh e-mail, called some like-minded colleagues, and then kicked his protest into high gear. He gave speeches in the student union. He held interviews with the student newspaper and radio station. He even carried a placard outside the administration building.

Honerman's protest succeeded in flushing out an explanation from the president's office. Steele had been given a three-month leave of absence due to a serious medical condition. The registrar had made no announcement because he had wanted to keep the matter confidential.

Four months later, Honerman was appointed the first director of the new racism center on campus, funded entirely by private donations. He received tenure the following year.

When it comes to confessions of racism, whites are like Italian soldiers during the waning days of World War II—they fall all over themselves to surrender. When it comes to race, self-indictment is about all whites can do to achieve any semblance of virtue.

A century and a half after the Civil War, and a half century after the rise of the civil rights movement, there are still constant accusations that America remains as pervasively racist as it ever was. The inherent racism of American society is a frequent theme in academic circles and among civil rights activists. Racial prejudice is said to be "rooted deeply in the whole structure of our society," requiring a "radical reconstruction of society itself."[1] A system of subtle racism continues to sustain "the pervasive power of white privilege" and condemn all but a select few to failure.[2] Racial inequality is "woven into the fabric of our lives," and as such is impervious to antidiscrimination laws.[3] As Professor Kimberle Crenshaw stated, "Racism is the central ideological underpinning of American society."[4] According to Cornel West, America is "chronically racist."[5] Derrick Bell argued that slavery is "a constant reminder" of what white America might do at any moment[6] and that the nation's racism persists despite the "absence of visible signs of discrimination."[7] AIDS has been depicted as a deliberate effort of white America to kill blacks, and the ACLU claims that a black driver who has not been harassed because of his race is an "aberration."[8]

According to America's self-appointed chroniclers of racism, nothing has changed since the days of the Ku Klux Klan and the night riders.

Increasingly, there is an automatic presumption of racism whenever a racial minority incurs some disadvantage. For instance, if an employer's percentage of minority employees is lower than the percentage of minorities in the general population, that employer is often presumed guilty of illegal discrimination.[9] As a former EEOC chairman explained: "We have vetoed the presumption of innocence."[10] Even companies that require their employees to speak English on the job are being sued for discrimination.[11]

Allegations of racism have become an almost instinctive reaction to legal investigations of minority officeholders. Such was the case with former Atlanta mayor Bill Campbell, who faced trial in 2006 on charges that he had turned city hall into a criminal enterprise during his eight-year term. The specific allegations included taking payoffs of more than $150,000, accepting more than $100,000 in illegal campaign contributions, filing false income tax returns, and receiving from city contractors such gifts as a $12,000 trip to Paris and nearly $10,000 worth of heating and air-conditioning equipment for his home. Furthermore, the same investigation that produced the indictment against Campbell had previously led to bribery, tax fraud, and perjury convictions of ten people, three of whom had worked in Campbell's administration. But the first line of defense for the former mayor was to attack the prosecution as racially motivated. Campbell had frequently employed this strategy while serving as mayor, making "a practice of discerning racial bias in his critics, whether they were newspaper writers, rival politicians or federal prosecutors."[12] And he employed this strategy even though, when he began his mayoral term, he had stated, "Atlanta has dealt with its racial concerns better than any other city in this country."[13]

ARGUMENTS OVER election results frequently reflect an automatic presumption of racism. If a white candidate runs against a black candidate, and the former wins, then the charge is inevitably made that racism influenced the election. Yet these charges ignore the flip-side reality. Many cities with white majorities—such as Charlotte, Denver, Kansas City, Minneapolis, New Haven, and Seattle—have elected black mayors. On the other hand, when cities of primarily black populations choose African American mayors, no accusations of racism are made. The 2006 mayoral election in New Orleans reflects this phenomenon. Ray Nagin, the black incumbent, was elected in 2002 "largely thanks to white support."[14] But after the city's mishandling of the Hurricane Katrina disaster, Nagin's support among whites declined substantially, and several strong white candidates decided to run against him. In response, Nagin transformed the campaign into a racial contest, in part with his provocative speech about New Orleans remaining a mostly black "chocolate city." Relying on racial solidarity, Nagin's campaign consultant said that in every previous election "black voters have voted for black candidates against a white candidate, [and] my feeling is they will do the same thing again."[15] As an influential black religious leader in New Orleans observed: "African Americans are usually very loyal to African American candidates. I've talked to some people who say, 'I don't care how bad the black is, he's better than any white.'"[16]

Allegations of white voter racism causing the defeat of black candidates also occurred in Milwaukee. After Marvin Pratt lost the city's mayoral election in April 2004, his wife echoed the sentiments of many supporters by proclaiming that "racism is alive and well in Milwaukee."[17] This charge was made even though white support for Pratt did not drop off until after news of Pratt's questionable financial dealings was revealed. Not only was Pratt delinquent in paying his bills, but he had been charged by the district attorney with five counts of campaign finance violations. Subsequent to these revelations, both the district attorney and the newspaper reporting the financial improprieties were charged with racism.

Some critics argue that whenever a black candidate is defeated, racism should be presumed unless there is "exceedingly persuasive proof . . . that some other factor accounted for the result."[18] It is also argued that since blacks tend to be more liberal on domestic issues, whites can couch their racially biased votes as mere political opposition. But this means that any conservative white who votes against a liberal black is presumed to have done so strictly for racist reasons.

The instinctive charges of racism are not confined to the political arena—it occurs across a wide social spectrum. When African American coaches are fired from professional sports teams, racism charges abound, even though coach firings are about as common as ticket price increases. Responding to the firings of black head coaches, Jesse Jackson has called the NFL "a culture driven by white supremacists."[19] But this charge ignores that approximately two-thirds of the players in the NFL are black. It also ignores the fact that black men were hired as head coaches in the first place; if the owners were racist, they presumably would not have even hired a black coach.

Sixth Avenue in Zephyrhills, Florida, runs all the way through town. But when the city council—at the request of a single black resident—changed the name of the street to Martin Luther King Jr. Avenue, an uproar ensued. The mostly white residents protested that the name change had been initiated by people who did not live on the street, that the council had acted without giving any public notice, that the new street name would impose on them the burden of changing their addresses, and that the name change disregarded the way the city was laid out on a grid of numbered streets and avenues. Despite these arguments, however, opponents to the name change were called racist. It's "racism, plain and simple," a resident of Zephyrhills said.[20]

When the Washington, D.C., school system decided to adopt an Afrocentric curriculum for its predominantly black student body, it hired a black consultant to develop the program. Subsequent to this appointment, the *Washington Post* revealed that the consultant's master's degree had been awarded by an unlicensed, unaccredited institution founded by the consultant herself. Despite requests from the media, the consultant would not name any of the courses offered by that institution, claiming that criticism of it and her was part of a "racist attack" directed by "white supremacists."[21]

The university designated a special black student dorm with a cafeteria that served a culturally compatible menu. The African American Studies Department moved to a prime campus location. More than 90 percent of the black students were on scholarship, and the academic advising office had two full-time advisers reserved exclusively for black students.

After the campus police raided a late-night party at the black student dorm, a surge of protest ensued. Demonstrations and marches were held; the university was discriminating against its minority students, the protest leaders claimed.

Actions by the police have been among those most racially suspect, and police departments are almost instinctively presumed to be enclaves of racist intolerance. This presumption, however, ignores the racial reality of contemporary police departments. In 2005, for instance, a majority of recruits to the New York City Police Academy were minorities; meanwhile, the entire New York City Police Department was only 53 percent white and declining every year.[22]

Arrests of black suspects by white police officers are often surrounded by charges of racism, and shootings of black suspects are almost always followed by allegations of racism. An example of such accusations occurred in February 2005, when Los Angeles community activists alleged racism in the shooting death of an African American youth. The youth had stolen a car, led police on a high-speed chase at four o'clock in the morning, and then, after being forced off the road, rammed his vehicle into the side of a stopped patrol car. At that point, the police officer fired at the car, killing the youth. In response, civil rights activists erupted in outrage, claiming that racism was the only motivator for the shooting.[23]

Just as a presumption of racism continues to linger even after police officers have been exonerated in the courts, so too does it linger in the aftermath of other exonerations. For instance, a series of black church burnings in the South during the 1990s was attributed to the work of white supremacists. Subsequent investigations, however, proved that the burnings were not racially motivated; they were either accidental or caused by other blacks. Yet to this day there is a continuing belief that the burnings were acts of racial hatred, just as there is a continuing belief, despite unquestioned proof to the contrary, that the 2000 election troubles in Florida were the result of racially targeted voter intimidation.

Allegations of racism can exist despite and sometimes even contrary to the evidence. Boxing champion Mike Tyson was accused of rape by a black beauty pageant contestant and was later convicted by a jury that included black members. Even so, filmmaker Spike Lee blamed racism for Tyson's conviction. According to Lee, the system was out to get Tyson because "he was making too much money" for an African American.[24] Similarly, when Washington, D.C., mayor Marion Barry was arrested on charges of purchasing and using crack cocaine, civil rights leaders alleged a racist conspiracy. Coming to the mayor's defense, Mary Frances Berry of the U.S. Commission on Civil Rights warned that "all black officials ought to assume that someone is after them because of racism."[25] Later, Marion Barry admitted his guilt.

This pattern of denial of guilt, allegations of racism against the accusers, and eventual confession or apology when confronted with the full force of the facts occurred in a 2006 controversy involving Congresswoman Cynthia McKinney. On March 29, 2006, McKinney scuffled with a police officer after she entered a congressional office building without her identification badge, circumvented a metal detector, and then refused to stop when requested three times to do so by a member of the Capitol Hill police. When the officer then tried to block McKinney's further entrance into the building, she struck him.[26] Subsequently, in response to a request by the Capitol Police for an arrest warrant against her, McKinney held a press conference and accused the police officer of racism and racial profiling. She also vowed to pursue a criminal investigation against the officer.[27] However, several days later, after a fuller airing of the facts and as federal prosecutors were considering criminal charges against her, McKinney publicly apologized for the incident.[28]

THERE HAS evolved an almost unlimited list of various kinds of racism. There is subconscious racism, subtle and covert racism,[29] neoracism,[30] metaracism (racism generated by modern technology),[31] process racism (referring to procedures that generate racially disparate outcomes),[32] kinetic racism,[33] malignant racism and benign racism,[34] cultural racism and enlightened racism,[35] "feel-good" racism,[36] and even racism "born of experiential ignorance."[37] "Representational racism" occurs when the media portrays a minority person in an unattractive setting, even if that setting is accurate.[38] And "institutional racism" is the term used for merit systems that fail to produce representational outcomes for minorities. Thus, racism is seen as an invisible hand, working in every corner of society to discriminate against minorities—the presumption being that, absent racism, all racial groups would be represented in all vocational categories according to their precise proportion within the general population.

Although fifty years of survey research has revealed a dramatic drop in overt racial prejudice, there is still a strident insistence, particularly in academia, that racism remains as pervasive as ever.[39] Of course, one way to support this claim is to expand the definition of racism. Another way is to derive new "foolproof" tests for racism designed to show the existence of racist attitudes. One such test is the so-called implicit associations test.[40] This test aims to reveal any negative images that an individual might associate with a particular minority group. For instance, if a white individual demonstrates a subconscious linkage between the words *blacks* and *poverty*, even though that individual might have just listened to a speech by a civil rights activist detailing the poverty conditions of many blacks, that individual can be categorized as harboring a racial prejudice. This approach rests on the assumption that racism permeates our subconscious minds, that whether we know it or not, we are all the helpless instruments of bias and prejudice. Essentially, the approach begins with the conclusion of racism and then goes through the motions of arriving at that conclusion.

Even when studies or statistics do not support a claim of racial discrimination, the assumption is still made that much discrimination goes unreported by minorities who simply don't want to cause trouble[41] or that whites simply "underreport" their racism on racial attitude surveys because they don't want to sound evil.[42] According to Derrick Bell, "Racial discrimination in the workplace is as vicious, if less obvious, than it was when employers posted signs: No Nigras Need Apply."[43] Racism apparently can also be found in white attitudes toward certain issues. Opposition to affirmative action, for instance, has been labeled a "sophisticated expression of racism."[44] Congressman Charles Rangel (D-NY) has equated attempts to eliminate racial preferences to Hitler's policies for extermination of the Jews.[45] Columnist Bob Herbert asserted that a New York City proposal to scale back remedial-reading programs at City College amounted to "ethnic cleansing."[46] Criticism of welfare policies has been called "code" for "white hostility to blacks."[47] Opponents of school busing are said to reflect a racism that is "deeply embedded" in society.[48] Even various aspects of the federal tax code, such as the marriage penalty and the limited deductibility of child-care expenses, are said to be racially biased against black families.[49]

Sometimes racism is equated simply with a failure to make special allowances based on racial characteristics. Consider, for instance, the situation of a police officer coming up to a group of young men who are hanging out at a street corner. Suddenly, one of the men (a black man) runs away, and the officer gives chase. Many judges would find that the officer had probable cause for pursuing the man and questioning him. But civil rights activists say that the mere running away at the sight of a police officer is not suggestive of any guilt, since young black men have ample reason to flee from the police. Therefore, to be free of racism, the police should make special considerations for the racial identity of whatever groups or individuals they encounter.[50]

A twenty-four-year-old black MBA graduate of the University of Indiana gave a testimonial to a civil rights group. He said he had experienced firsthand the racist expectations of the corporate world. After receiving his degree, he had interviewed with one of the largest corporations in America for a position in its management training program. He knew how the game was played, he told the group, but to him it was just a racist game through and through. So he appeared for the interview in the same outfit he was wearing now—sneakers, baggy jeans, an extra-long football jersey, and a baseball cap. He never had a second interview, he told the group.

Clothes are like an extension of one's skin, someone said during the reception following the talk. To have a prejudice against clothes was akin to having a prejudice against skin color. But then, how many recording executives would give an audition to a punk rock singer who shows up in wing-tipped shoes, white oxford shirt, red tie, neatly combed hair, and a Bible in his hand?

The growing presumption of racial discrimination has led to an increasing presumption of other kinds of discrimination as well. Like shoots from a tree trunk, discrimination is branching out from race. A recent report by Amnesty International alleges that one in three Americans is at high risk of being victimized because he or she belongs to a racial, ethnic, or religious group whose members are commonly targeted by police for unlawful stops and searches.[51] One in three! At this rate, it won't be long until the people being discriminated against will constitute the majority. Likewise, a report by the Gay, Lesbian and Straight Education Network concluded that 84 percent of America's schools are "unsafe" for gay students, defining an unsafe school to include any in which students engage in teasing and name-calling.[52] Indeed, the discrimination mentality has become so pervasive that even when artwork by men is sold for a greater price than different work by women artists, discrimination is alleged.[53]

This exaltation of the victim often results in the escalation of petty disappointments into dramatic, victim-making injustices, such as when a Miss Colorado claimed that her titleholder's contract, which required her to be available at all pageant-affiliated events, amounted to "a form of slavery."[54] Or when a heavyset man in Chicago filed a complaint with the Minority Rights Division of the U.S. Attorney's Office, alleging that his rights were being violated because the seats at McDonald's restaurants were too small for him. The man said he was "being discriminated against no less than blacks, Mexicans, Latins, Asians, or women."[55]

A lawsuit filed by the Welsh American Legal Defense Fund against several prominent newspapers and television stations exemplifies the trend of finding new kinds of discrimination to assert. Viewing the media's use of the verb to welsh as a slur on the Welsh people, the plaintiffs contended that the media "degraded the Welsh and Welsh-Americans in a manner in which the same media modernly do not, and dare not, defame any other ethnic group or nationality."[56]

A San Francisco couple sued Northwest Airlines for kicking them off a flight because of their verbal harassment of other passengers—the result, the couple claimed, of a disorder that caused them to scream obscenities involuntarily. They charged the airline with illegally discriminating against them because of their disability.

Discrimination lawsuits have also been extended to cover allegations of "lookism"—the practice of preferring the pretty over the plain. According to a spokesperson for the American Civil Liberties Union, ugly people need to be protected against the discrimination caused by lookism: "People don't realize how pervasive the preference for the beautiful is in our society, starting with teachers who give attractive children better grades."[57]

The assertion of discrimination claims is becoming so widespread that an almost competitive spirit has arisen among alleged victims.

When New Jersey school officials proposed a showing of *Schindler's List* in the state's high schools, minority groups attacked the decision, saying that the emphasis on the Holocaust elevated Jewish suffering while ignoring the injustices endured by other racial groups.

At a social outing during a weeklong sales visit to an important customer, an employee of a Fortune 500 corporation was overheard making a racial slur. This slur was reported the next day on a local radio call-in show, and news of it quickly reached corporate headquarters. Within twenty-four hours of the slur, a termination notice was sent via e-mail. Three days later, the corporation was served with a racial discrimination suit. As it turned out, in its rush to punish the racist, the corporation had fired the wrong person. The man who had made the slur had a common last name, which was shared by another employee of the corporation. That other employee was black.

The antidiscrimination mind-set has become so ingrained in American culture that it can justify nearly any cost to be paid to combat perceived infringements on individual rights, even when those infringements don't always involve race. This can be seen in the due process revolution that has occurred within America's public school system. As a result of the Supreme Court decision in *Goss v. Lopez*, students now possess due process protections for minor, day-to-day impositions of routine school discipline. In the aftermath of *Goss*, even in-school detention can be subject to a court challenge. According to a 2004 Public Agenda poll, 78 percent of teachers noted that students were quick to remind them that they could sue in response to disciplinary action.[58] But without the ability to impose a minimal level of discipline, educators can hardly be expected to teach students the importance of adhering to basic societal norms and behaviors. During a two-month period in 2004, for instance, seventy-six fires were set by students in the Baltimore public school system. And on one day in October, firefighters received more than ten calls from Baltimore schools regarding deliberately set fires.[59]

To VIEW the extent to which racism is presumed in society, it is particularly instructive to look at the world of academia. If there is any place in America that is sensitive to race issues, it is higher education. Universities have led the crusade for affirmative action programs and speech codes outlawing racially derogatory statements.[60] They have created whole new subjects of academic study to accommodate new racial interests and sensitivities—for example, African American and hip-hop studies. In *The Burden of Bad Ideas: How Modern Intellectuals Misshape Our Society*, Heather MacDonald reveals how high schools try to boost minority self-esteem by teaching courses in "ghetto culture," including such subjects as break dancing and graffiti painting. For the 2001–2 academic year, the University of California, Santa Barbara, listed sixty-two different courses under "Chicano Studies."[61] And while the history department listed thirteen courses on Latin and Chicano studies, there were no specific courses devoted to the Revolutionary War or World War II.[62]

Aside from creating subject areas that cater to various racial sensitivities, even the manner in which subjects are taught has been modified. In the nation's law schools, for instance, deconstructionists seek to replace the use of rationality, claiming that it promotes white supremacy, with that of "life stories" that are apparently more compatible with minority viewpoints and thought processes. According to one law scholar, critical race theorists, simply by delivering an unrelenting message of victimization, are able to publish dubious articles that fail to meet the prevailing academic standards of scholarship.[63]

At universities across the county, scores of minority race-based organizations (like black fraternities) receive huge financial subsidies. Each year, more than one hundred million dollars in race-based financial aid is distributed by colleges and universities.[64] In professional schools alone, 10 percent of all available scholarship money goes exclusively to minority students.[65] At Harvard University, all minority graduate students receive full tuition, room, and board, irrespective of their financial need.[66] The Afro American Studies program at Harvard was

45

given a forty-million-dollar endowment, more than two dozen professors, and a twenty-five-million-dollar office space, even though the department had a mere twenty-six undergraduate majors.[67]

Curriculum standards also reflect the racial sensitivities of educators. The *National Standards for United States History,* a federally funded curriculum guide outlining what students should know about American history that is backed by the American Federation of Teachers and the National Education Association, reveals the kind of priority given to the subject of discrimination.[68] Harriet Tubman, the African American who helped organize the pre–Civil War underground railroad, was cited six times in the *Standards,* whereas Lincoln's Gettysburg Address was mentioned only once in passing. While the 1848 Seneca Falls convention on women's rights was heavily emphasized, the inventions of Thomas Edison and Alexander Graham Bell were not even listed. And though vehemently opposing any emphasis on Western civilization in the *Standards,* the American Historical Association praised the *Standards'* focus on the "achievements and grandeur" of Mansa Musa's court in West Africa. Essentially, the *National Standards* incorporates a "victim" view of American history, portraying it as a story of oppression and discrimination. It sees the defining identity of America not in the promise of opportunity embodied in the Statue of Liberty but in isolated episodes of restrictive immigration laws.

This obsession with victimhood, however, can exert a distorting influence on historical truth. For instance, regarding the plight of Native Americans, historian Glenn Morris states that Christopher Columbus was "a murderer, a rapist [and] the architect of a policy of genocide that continues today."[69] Similar distortions have arisen within the field of African American studies. In striving to improve black students' self-esteem, for instance, Afro-centric history claims that Africans were in the New World even before Columbus, that ancient Greece stole its politics and philosophy from Africa, and that European culture is nothing more than a bastardized version of African culture.

The flip side of academia's racial sensitivity is its hesitancy to criticize or discipline racial minorities. When staff members of a conservative student newspaper engaged in an argument with a black professor at Dartmouth that resulted in a shouting-and-pushing match between students and the professor, the university found only the students guilty of disorderly conduct. The university president also criticized the student journalists for "poisoning the intellectual environment."[70] At Columbia University, black student demonstrators who forcibly occupied the administration building received no punishment or discipline.[71] And at the University of Massachusetts, a five-day occupation of the African American Studies building by 250 minority students ended only after the university agreed to many of the students' demands.[72]

University faculty and administrators tend to deal harshly with student actions that oppose certain "racially correct" positions. Throughout 2003 and 2004, for instance, a surge of student protests erupted against affirmative action. Students at UCLA and the University of Michigan sponsored bake sales to make their point: for white students a cookie cost one dollar, but for black students the cost was much less. Despite the peaceful nature of these bake sales, however, they were banned at several schools by indignant administrators.[73] Likewise, university officials have tried to shut down conservative student publications that oppose certain racial policies. Cornell's dean of students stood alongside student activists as they burned copies of the *Cornell Review*, which had run an article criticizing Ebonics. And when a California Polytechnic State University white student tried to post a flyer advertising a lecture by a black conservative, he was stopped by campus police, who described the student in their report as "a suspicious white male passing out literature of an offensive racial nature."[74]

Despite this solicitous and accommodating mind-set of higher education, academics and civil rights activists alike claim that college campuses are the sites of pervasive racism. As one scholar writes, "Racism on campus is real and substantial."[75] There is a wealth of testimony by legal scholars regarding the racial discrimination that has existed, and which continues to exist, in the nation's institutions of higher education.[76] T. Alexander Aleinikoff states that racism is "widespread, deeply ingrained, passed from generation to generation."[77] As Aleinikoff argues, what needs to be changed is "the institutional culture" of universities—a culture that is "overwhelmingly white" and which limits to whites any real access to social power.[78] Harvard professor Cornel West, who received a salary in excess of three hundred thousand dollars and held one of only twenty prestigious "university professor" appointments at Harvard, claims that "dignity is all a black person in America has."[79] According to Professor Charles Lawrence, racism is an "illness that affects almost everyone."[80] A black psychology class at San Francisco State University teaches that "white psychology is inherently racist."[81] And Harvard professor Lawrence Bobo teaches his students that African Americans' problems are permanent, "short of a revolutionary rending of the national fabric."[82]

Some academics contend that race relations are actually more problematic in higher education than elsewhere. One legal scholar states that "the subtle institutional racism and white cultural bias that pervade the campus infringes on black students' right to equal enjoyment of their civil right to an education."[83] Even liberal faculty members are described as helplessly racist: though they try to deny their historical connections to racial supremacy, "they often exhibit colonialist impulses when writing about race without even knowing it."[84] Scholars argue that there are unequivocal signs "indicating that racial equality has not yet found its way to many institutions of higher education" and that there is "ample evidence that there exists some form of discrimination" even at some of the nation's elite law schools.[85]

Universities and law schools are accused of subtly reinforcing racial stereotypes through the use of discriminatory testing and admissions standards.[86] As critical race theory proclaims, the standards used to measure achievement in higher education are a "gate built by a white male hegemony that requires a password in the white man's voice for passage."[87] According to the NAACP, institutions of higher education "have been complacent in perpetuating racial disadvantage" and for "far too long the doors to those positions [within higher education] have been shut to Negroes."[88]

When black poet Amiri Baraka was denied tenure at Rutgers University, he accused his fellow professors and administrators of being Nazis and Ku Klux Klansmen in disguise.[89] After St. Mary's College threatened to terminate Reginald Savage because he had been absent for months, teaching elsewhere, Savage claimed to be the victim of campus racism; colleagues, however, said that Savage habitually accused anyone who disagreed with him as being a racist.[90]

Even collegiate athletics have been accused of having a "continued presence of racism."[91] The alleged evidence of this racism includes "positional segregation on the playing field," such as blacks being benched in games more quickly than whites.[92] In addition, rules limiting a coach's contact with student-athletes are seen as racist, because minority students who come from single-parent homes are said to need strong father figures for guidance. These rules allegedly result in the "disproportionately high African American involvement in substantial scandals over the past thirty years."[93] Furthermore, the large numbers of black student-athletes reinforce the stereotype "that blacks are better suited to physical activities than to intellectual pursuits."[94] But this is a contradiction in terms, since many young black males choose a life in athletics over one in academia. In addition, the charge that not enough academic standards are placed on black athletes, allowing them to go through college without getting a degree, likewise ignores the just as frequently made charge that academic standards imposed on black athletes are racist because they increase the risk that they might be placed on academic probation, thereby jeopardizing their athletic career. This resembles the more general claim that racism exists because minority students lag "substantially behind whites."[95] Yet whenever the attempt is made to impose rigorous educational standards on all students, many civil rights activists claim racism—for example, that black students should not be held to standards that will doom them to poor performance.

The continued accusations of racism within the nation's institutions of higher education at some point seem only to testify to the futility of remedial action. But there is no group in society more committed to racial diversity than the nation's higher education faculty. In general, university faculties have been strongly supportive of affirmative action.[96] In *Grutter v. Bollinger*,[97] which upheld the University of Michigan Law School's race-conscious admissions policy, ninety-one colleges and universities filed briefs in support of the University of Michigan; not one college or university filed a brief opposing affirmative action.[98] A recent survey of five hundred law school faculty members found that an overwhelming majority supported efforts to achieve diversity in the classroom.[99] Many even go so far as to argue vigorously for aggressive implementation of affirmative action programs.[100] According to a former chancellor at the University of California at Berkeley, a university without affirmative action is akin to an educational apartheid that is "almost as pervasive and insidious as the strictest segregation [that once existed] in South Africa."[101]

As far back as 1964, the American Association of Law Schools began exploring the use of racial admissions preferences.[102] By 1968, a number of law schools were either commencing or accelerating their racial preference programs.[103] Even after *Bakke* outlawed racial quotas, law schools continued to operate unacknowledged quota programs; indeed, "few American law schools feel that they have any meaningful choice but to engage in covert practices that, if made explicit, would probably not survive judicial scrutiny."[104] Consequently, the number of black first-year law students attending schools other than the historically black schools "rose from about two hundred in 1964–1965 to perhaps five hundred in 1968–1969, eight hundred in 1969–1970, and seventeen hundred in 1973–1974."[105] Continuing this increase, the period from

1985 to 1994 saw a 100 percent rise in the number of first-year black law students.[106] As one commentator notes, an entrenched system of racial preferences is "a characteristic of legal education as a whole."[107] Indeed, a proposal made to the ABA Section on Legal Education and Admissions in February 2006 requires that all law schools seeking to maintain ABA accreditation adopt a system of racial preferences in both hiring and admissions, regardless of any federal, state, or local laws prohibiting such policies.[108]

At the conclusion of a three-day conference on racism, the president of the college gave a speech in which he strongly reaffirmed the college's commitment to affirmative action. Joining him onstage were all the deans and vice presidents. They nodded as the president issued his proclamation of support for affirmative action.

During the subsequent question-and-answer session, a female student suggested that, since everyone was in support of affirmative action and since everyone recognized the value of diversity in the university's administration, 40 percent of the all-white, all-male contingent of deans and vice presidents should resign so that minorities could be hired to fill those slots, thus immediately achieving the desired diversity. The student received no direct answer to her suggestion.

In a way, the academic community has enjoyed a free ride on the racial-virtue train. Faculty members have been eager advocates of affirmative action, and yet, because of tenure, they have had to incur no costs or burdens in the social crusade for diversity. So by supporting affirmative action, white male faculty members can ease whatever guilt or discomfort they might feel on racial issues while at the same time incurring no risk of being forced to suffer any economic hardship themselves.

Surveys have shown that university faculty tend to be "ideologically and politically far more liberal, Democratic, statist, and secular than other Americans."[109] One study of several universities found that nearly

90 percent of liberal arts professors were Democrats.[110] According to another survey of more than a thousand academics, Democratic professors outnumber Republicans by at least seven to one in the humanities and social sciences.[111] In a separate study of voter registration records, a nine-to-one ratio of Democrats to Republicans was found on the faculties of Berkeley and Stanford. The ratio was even more lopsided among the younger professors: 183 Democrats to 6 Republicans.[112] Another study showed that liberal-leaning professors outnumber conservative-leaning professors at Brown University by 54 to 3; at the University of Chicago, it was 116 to 5; at UCLA, it was 141 to 9; and at Syracuse, 50 to 2.[113] This compares with a 1995 study that reflects a similar disparity: at Cornell, 171 Democrats to 7 Republicans; and at Stanford, 163 Democrats to 17 Republicans.[114] According to one Harvard professor, "We have 60 members in the department of government [and] maybe three are Republicans."[115]

This ideological tilt can also be found in the academy's political donations. During the 2004 campaign season, for instance, 97 percent of Harvard University's employees' political donations went to the Democratic Party.[116] At Cornell, the figure was 93 percent; at Dartmouth, 97 percent; and at Yale, 93 percent.[117] Employees at the University of California gave more money to John Kerry's presidential campaign than did workers at any other business or institution, including such Fortune 500 corporations as Microsoft and Time Warner. In second place among givers to the Kerry campaign were the employees of Harvard University. George Bush, on the other hand, had no universities in his top-twenty list of employee donations.

Yet despite their strong liberal beliefs, the insulation of tenured faculty members from any adverse effects of affirmative action programs casts a certain suspicion on their arguments in support of such programs. Indeed, most of the Supreme Court's affirmative action decisions have involved not the professional or intellectual classes but occupations such as police officers and firefighters.[118] The bulk of the judicial affirmative action docket has been directed to, as the Court once described it, "the work of the manual laborer, as distinguished from that of the professional or, indeed, of any class whose toil is that of the brain."[119]

The racial views of academia are also suspect because of their almost blind adherence to the discrimination mind-set. Free-ranging inquiry and open debate are often stifled by immediate allegations of discrimination. This was particularly evident in a controversy involving Harvard president Lawrence Summers. In January 2005, during a conference organized by the National Bureau of Economic Research, Summers questioned whether discrimination was entirely responsible for the relative lack of female professors in science and engineering at America's elite universities.[120] He suggested that researchers investigate additional reasons for why women are underrepresented in the hard sciences. Those reasons include the possibility that women are not as interested as men in putting in the eighty-hour weeks required by such positions and that men have more intrinsic aptitude for the hard sciences.[121] Repeatedly throughout the speech, Summers admitted that he could be wrong and challenged researchers to study his propositions. Thus, his comments to a scholarly audience were intended to prompt the kind of orthodoxy-challenging debate for which universities are supposed to exist. But instead, his speech "touched the third rail of contemporary university life by questioning one of the hallowed tenets of the victimization industry: Deliberate discrimination explains all inequality of result, precluding free discussion of other theories."[122]

Members of the academic audience reacted with outrage. Biologist Nancy Hopkins fled the room before Summers finished speaking. "My heart was pounding and my breath was shallow; I was extremely upset," she said.[123] As Hopkins later explained, she would have "either blacked out or thrown up" if she had stayed.[124] And yet virtually all academic literature on gender, IQ, and aptitude reveals significant differences between men and women.[125] On average, women perform better on verbal tests while men show greater visual-spatial capabilities. Though boys outnumber girls in remedial-reading classes, they are also more likely to outnumber girls among the most gifted in math and science.[126] Despite this scientific evidence, however, the accusations of discrimination flew fast and furious at Summers. Even his own faculty reacted with a vote of no-confidence. But as Charles Murray notes, the intellectual elites are "living a lie," doggedly asserting that "all groups of people are equal in all respects."[127] And this lie is perpetuated by the taboo against openly discussing differences for fear of being called racist. It is a taboo that "has crippled our ability to explore almost any topic that involves the different ways in which groups of people respond to the world around them—which mean almost every political, social, or economic topic of any complexity."[128]

The discrimination mind-set in higher education often causes a reflexive siding with the perceived underdog and a corresponding racist attack on the more powerful. This inclination is illustrated by the annual conference of the Palestine Solidarity Movement, held each year at a major American university. These academic conferences coalesce around rabid accusations of Israeli racism. An organizer of the 2002 conference wrote that the Palestinian plight made him "want to strap a bomb to his chest and kill those Zionist racists."[129] A speaker at the 2004 conference openly called for terrorist attacks against Israeli youth. Another lecturer claimed that Israel was "the greatest abuser of human rights" in the world.[130] After the conference, a media dialogue ensued in which the anti-Israeli rhetoric intensified. One writer in the Duke student newspaper denounced Jews as "the most privileged 'minority' group in the United States" and bemoaned the "shocking overrepresentation" of Jews in academia[131]; another blamed the Jews for the outbreak of World War II. But aside from this hostile rhetoric, perhaps the most shocking aspect of the PSM conference and its aftermath is that it took place with at least the tacit endorsement of mainstream academia.

THREE

Awash in ContradictiOns

THE DETROIT City Council passed a proposal to use taxpayer funds to create a racially exclusive business district aimed at aiding black entrepreneurs.[1] The plan, dubbed "Africa Town," stems from the premise that immigrants from Latin America, Asia, and the Middle East are "stealing jobs and resources from native blacks."[2] Although Detroit's Asian and Arab residents angrily denounced the plan as reverse racism, supporters argued that the color-blind approach was just an excuse to do nothing.[3]

Civil rights advocates claim that Detroit is more segregated than any other large metropolis in the nation.[4] They claim that the city's public schools are the most segregated in the country.[5] The Justice Department allegedly files more housing discrimination lawsuits in Detroit than anywhere else.[6] Black Detroiters blame their troubles on institutional racism, even though blacks control every institution in the city, including the mayor's office. Indeed, the city's population is more than 80 percent black. Consequently, "Africa Town" hardly seems to fit the affirmative action model in which public aid is given to an underrepresented minority.

Similar to the "Africa Town" proposal is a plan being considered by the U.S. Senate that would establish a separate, race-based government for native Hawaiians.[7] This new government would create a racially exclusive domain for the lineal descendants of native Hawaiians. Such a plan, however, would more or less undo what the Civil War accomplished: it would allow a race-based government to effectively secede from the United States and would undermine the notions of equality enshrined in the Declaration of Independence and the Gettysburg Address.

The current state of confusion over racial matters is often attributed to implementation of affirmative action models. In principle, a democratic society should turn a blind eye to the race, color, creed, and gender of its citizens. Rewards should be granted according to individual merit, not skin color. This color-blind approach, as advocated by Martin Luther King Jr., provided a unifying energy to the civil rights movement. It not only empowered racial minorities seeking social justice, it also inspired the larger culture to mobilize against racism. With its clarity and simplicity, the color-blind ideal served an important educational role: it revealed the inherent wrong of racism while at the same time showing the path toward reform.

Currently, however, color-blindness is said to be just another form of racism. It is supposedly a tool with which whites can maintain a status quo while blacks are trapped in an unequal position. It is said to be the rock behind which racists hide when opposing policies such as affirmative action. And yet, as the color-blind approach falls from favor, racial divisions in society appear to be deepening, with racial segregation intensifying.[8] Studies have suggested that throughout the 1990s, housing and education in America actually became more racially segregated.[9]

Jason was a new professor in the history department. He had only one African American student in his diplomatic history class, and tomorrow that student was scheduled to give a presentation.

Every student in class had to make a presentation, but Jason was anguishing over how to handle this student. If he was tough on the student, as he had been with the other students, it could look like he was being racially insensitive and not taking into account the student's unique background. On the other hand, if Jason was too lenient on the student, it could appear as if he had lower expectations for that student, as if he didn't believe the student could compete with the others.

Jason sat at his kitchen table and checked his notes from the two-day conference on racial sensitivity he had attended as part of his orientation. It was a long night.

Even though affirmative action is often blamed for the racial confusion plaguing America, something much larger is at the root of all the uncertainty and hostility. Racism has become a sin of no clear definition—and since the nature of the sin is unknown, the remedy or retribution is equally unknown. Most whites have no idea how to bring about racial reconciliation, nor do they know what precise duties or remedies they owe to racial minorities, nor even to what extent they are presently guilty of racist attitudes or behavior. Likewise, America's racial minorities are uncertain about what they should expect from the majority and what they as individuals should be responsible for and what the larger society owes them.

America has become locked in a tunnel-visioned racial mentality that reaches back to the days of slavery. The racial sensitivities that have evolved since then between whites and blacks are causing conflict and confusion elsewhere with other racial and ethnic groups. For instance, the attempt by census officials to require Hispanics to characterize their racial identity as either black or white evokes outrage. Elimination of the census category "some other race," which was the category chosen by 42 percent of Hispanics in the 2000 census, has stirred a furious debate among Hispanics, many of whom "embrace a kaleidoscope of racial identities that transcends traditional notions of black and white."[10] But the reason census officials are trying to eliminate the "some other race" category is because it forces statisticians to guess at the precise racial group of the individual. Wrong guesses could lead to inaccuracies in the data used to monitor civil rights enforcement, which could then cover up the amount of racial discrimination occurring in society, according to the Joint Center for Political and Economic Studies, a research group that studies issues of concern to blacks. In other words, mistakenly categorizing Hispanics as whites could give an inaccurate picture of the number of minorities in a certain area, which could influence electoral redistricting decisions in ways contrary to the interests of blacks.

Identity confusion has also occurred with the racial categorization of Asian Americans. At times, they are classified as racial minorities, but in the context of affirmative action, Asian Americans are usually categorized as whites. This is because affirmative action often hurts Asian Americans. After California abandoned racial preferences in university admissions, for instance, the number of Asian Americans in the first-year class at UCLA Law School jumped 81 percent.[11] And if Asian Americans had been counted as minorities, the total minority enrollment at UCLA following the elimination of racial preferences actually increased.[12] Thus, as Stephan Thernstrom notes, affirmative action supporters are turning Asians into "honorary whites."[13]

Amid their own maze of contradictory politically correct rules, universities are riddled with double standards regarding race. And these double standards begin the moment a student applies for admission. While the application form declares the university's commitment to evaluate candidates "without regard to race, gender, religion, ethnicity, or national origin" on page 1, it then informs applicants on page 2 that it is advantageous to mention if they belong to certain designated racial or ethnic groups.

A white student at the University of Florida publicized the mission statement of an organization for which he claimed to have sought recognition from the Student Government Association. After being besieged by accusations of racism, the student revealed that he had simply taken a publication from the Black Student Union and changed the word *black* to *white* each time it appeared.[14]

When an unexpectedly large freshman class arrived at Wesleyan University, the university tried to fill nine empty spaces at the Malcolm X student residential house with whites, but it backed down when black students objected to living with anyone of another race. The white students were then moved to the basement of the philosophy building.[15]

After members of a Georgia State University fraternity showed up in blackface at an off-campus hip-hop theme party, a black student group passed out a flyer depicting the fraternity as a group of Ku Klux Klansman about to lynch a black man. The university demanded that each group apologize to the other, but only the fraternity had to implement a diversity training program and agree never to permit any of its members to paint their faces again, even though face painting may well be protected by the First Amendment. The black student group, on the other hand, had to make no such promises regarding future accusations of lynching and KKK affinity.

It was a tradition on campus. Every Halloween, a talent show was held, with the ticket proceeds going to charity. One year, two different fraternities decided to team up on an act that mimicked an old vaudeville show. One fraternity—a primarily white fraternity—put on whiteface and performed a demeaning impersonation of Jimmy Durante. The other fraternity—a primarily black fraternity—donned blackface and did a similar kind of impersonation of Louis Armstrong. In the audience was a visitor to campus, a guest lecturer in the law school. The next day, he went to the president's office and demanded that the "racists in the black face" be appropriately disciplined for engaging in racially belittling behavior.

Having lost the moral clarity and simplicity of the color-blind ideal, racism in America has turned onto a one-way street. When a white police officer kills a black youth, the officer is immediately vulnerable to charges of racism. But black policemen who kill white suspects are placed under no such suspicion. When mobs of whites attack blacks, it is seen as further evidence of white bigotry. But when mobs of blacks attack whites, it is downplayed as a natural reaction to decades of racist exploitation. This double-standard approach to racism is exemplified through a comparison of the twin cities of Minneapolis and St. Paul, Minnesota. During the late 1990s, Minneapolis had a black mayor and a white police chief, whereas St. Paul had a white mayor and a black police chief. Whenever an issue of police brutality or police racism arose in St. Paul, the mayor became the object of criticism. But when the same kind of issues arose in Minneapolis, the police chief bore the brunt of public outrage.

In 2003, a twenty-four-year-old black man led police on a seventeen-mile high-speed chase, which ended only after the man crashed into a squad car. The pursuing deputies then surrounded the man and ordered him to lay down on the ground. Approaching the man, one of the deputies momentarily put a restraining foot on the man's neck. Almost immediately afterward, the NAACP called a meeting to denounce police brutality. At the meeting, the sheriff of Milwaukee County asked the crowd if they thought the offending deputy was racist. The verdict was a resounding "yes." Then the sheriff held up a photo of the deputy, who was black.[16]

The subject of crime and race is a subject inundated with confusion and contradiction. A common accusation is that, because of racist police attitudes, black drivers are much more likely to be stopped than are whites. But according to a 2002 survey conducted by the Bureau of Justice Statistics, an identical proportion of white, black, and Hispanic drivers—9 percent—were stopped by the police in the previous year.[17] Moreover, the stop rate for blacks was actually lower during the day, when police can more easily determine a driver's race than at night. Furthermore, law-enforcement statistics compiled in New Jersey show that black state troopers stop the same proportion of black drivers as do their white colleagues.[18]

The high incidence of black arrests and the high proportion of blacks in the nation's prison population are also attributed to racism. But this completely ignores the possibility that certain crimes are committed more frequently by black perpetrators—a possibility that has been factually verified by a number of studies. Michael Tonry of the University of Minnesota Law School has found that the higher levels of arrests and incarceration of African Americans are the result of higher levels of crime, not racial bias.[19] A research study commissioned by the New Jersey attorney general reports that, on the New Jersey Turnpike, blacks are twice as likely to speed as white drivers, are even more dominant among drivers exceeding ninety miles per hour, and yet are actually stopped less than their speeding behavior would predict.[20] In New York City, though blacks make up 25 percent of the population, victims of violent crime identify their assailants as black 62 percent of the time.[21] Similar records in Hartford, Connecticut, show that while whites are nearly 30 percent of the population, they commit only 7 percent of the violent crimes.[22] On the other hand, Department of Justice data shows that conviction rates for blacks are actually lower than for whites in twelve of the fourteen most serious felony categories, including robbery, rape, and assault.[23]

The U.S. Justice Department's annual victimization surveys, based on reports by crime victims unlikely to lie in their descriptions of the offenders they want brought to justice, suggest that blacks currently commit violent crimes at a much higher rate than whites.[24] Moreover, if racism were responsible for the large number of blacks in prison, one would expect the racial discrepancies between blacks and whites to have decreased over time, since no one argues that the criminal justice system is more racist now than it was thirty or fifty years ago. But, in fact, a larger proportion of blacks are in prison today than at virtually any other time in this and the last century.[25] Even Jesse Jackson recognized this problem when he admitted, "There is nothing more painful for me than to walk down the street and hear footsteps and start to think about robbery, and then see it's somebody white and feel relieved."[26] This view is echoed by African American scholar Johnetta Cole, who states that "one of the most painful admissions" she hears from black women is that they are "afraid of their own people."[27]

WITH RESPECT to racism on the part of minorities, contradictions abound. The racial atmosphere in the United States often reflects the assumption that whites have a monopoly on racist behavior. As Malcolm X once observed, whites are incorrigibly racist, to the point of being satanic. During a recent hip-hop political convention, one of the workshops included "How to Get Stupid White Men Out of Office."[28] But as America becomes increasingly diverse, racial tensions are likewise occurring in a plethora of settings, including those in which whites are not even involved. In Plainfield, New Jersey, at least seventeen Hispanic men have been beaten to death by gangs of black men. Even though city leaders say that racism was not the cause of the deaths, substantial evidence exists indicating that the brutal beatings were in fact racially motivated.[29] Plainfield is a community in which African Americans, the dominant racial group, complain that Hispanics are "taking over" and that Hispanics speak only Spanish and rarely hire blacks. In response, Hispanics claim that blacks are jealous of their economic success and are "out to get them" and assert that the police are not doing enough to protect them from black violence. A similar kind of black hostility to Hispanics has been revealed in New Orleans, where the cleanup of Hurricane Katrina resulted in an influx of Mexican workers. As Mayor Ray Nagin, an African American, remarked in response to this influx: "How do I ensure that New Orleans is not overrun by Mexican workers?"[30]

Although having long decried racial stereotypes as reflective of racist attitudes, many inner-city blacks who chafe under the economic successes of Korean businesses attribute that success to the moral deficiencies of Koreans. They succeed, the argument goes, because they are willing to adopt vicious and underhanded practices that are beneath African American ethical standards. African Studies professor Anderson Thompson condemns "the miserable Asiatic" who lives like a "parasite on the black consumer."[31] Similarly, rapper Ice Cube calls for violence against Korean merchants because they are "Oriental one-penny-counting m[—]s."[32]

A survey conducted by the National Conference of Christians and Jews finds that many minority groups harbor much more hostile attitudes toward each other than do whites.[33] For example, 49 percent of blacks and 68 percent of Asians say that Hispanics "tend to have bigger families than they can support." Forty-six percent of Hispanics and 42 percent of blacks say that Asian Americans are "unscrupulous, crafty and devious in business." And 53 percent of Asians and 51 percent of Hispanics declare that blacks "are more likely to commit crimes and violence."[34]

Surveys also show that African Americans are nearly twice as likely as whites to hold anti-Semitic views.[35] Harry Allen, an agent for the rap group Public Enemy, claims that his denunciations of Jews are not racist. "Only white people can be racist," he explains, "and I am not white."[36] Similarly, Sister Souljah declares: "You can't call me or any black person anywhere in the world a racist—we don't have the power to do to white people what white people have done to us; and even if we did, we don't have that low-down dirty nature."[37] Whitney Young of the National Urban League states in his book *Beyond Racism* that blacks' antiwhite attitudes cannot be equated with white racism because that would be "to equate the bitterness of the victim with the evil that oppresses him."[38]

Philip was a college basketball coach who was having more problems off the court than on. One of his players had just been suspended for letting his grades slip below the required minimum, and Philip was criticized by a civil rights group for not providing sufficient academic support to his minority players. But two years earlier, Philip had been sanctioned because one of his players had received too much help—a tutor had written most of the research papers herself. The criticism then had been that Philip didn't treat his white and black players equally, that he thought his black players needed extra help.

The argument is often made that the poor academic performances of black children are due to pervasive racism in the schools. Yet there is significant evidence pointing to an array of other responsible factors. In *No Excuses: Closing the Racial Gap in Learning*, Abigail Thernstrom argues that the real culprit behind the academic problems of African American children is an inadequate and unresponsive public educational system. As DePaul University professor William Sampson explains in *Black Student Achievement*, neither race nor income nor neighborhood is responsible for the poor academic performances of black children—it is the parents who are responsible. Furthermore, accusations of racism ignore all the special preferences given to racial minorities. The National Merit Scholarship Board, for instance, became so self-conscious about the low number of African Americans winning college scholarships that it created an entirely separate program exclusively for blacks.[39]

A study conducted in the Des Moines public schools revealed that black students are suspended at much higher rates than students of other ethnic groups.[40] In elementary schools, black students received 37 percent of the suspensions, even though they made up only 15 percent of the enrollment. To many, the cause for such high rates of disciplinary action is simply racism. As one thirteen-year-old summed it up, "Teachers are racist." But many other school districts across the country have similarly high suspension rates for black students.[41] There is also evidence that black children disproportionately come from troubled homes—and such domestic environments often lead to behavioral problems at school.

John Ogbu, a Nigerian-born anthropologist at the University of California, has studied black underachievement in America's public schools and has concluded that blacks' educational failures arise from "a kind of cultural orientation which defines academic learning in school as 'acting white.'"[42] He suggests that the most effective way to improve black academic performance lies not in the continued allegations of racism but in the black community's changing its own attitudes toward education. In his book, *Black American Students*, Ogbu reveals his findings on black academic performance in the racially integrated, upper-middle-class Cleveland suburb of Shaker Heights. During his study of Shaker Heights, he found that even though black students and their parents did not complain of cultural racism, the parents had nonetheless taught their children to be cynical toward white-controlled institutions. Reflecting that cynicism, nearly half of the black students in Shaker Heights looked down on highly educated black adults as having given up their racial identity to become "white representatives."

According to Ogbu, middle-class black students are no different from lower-class black students in their ambivalence about academic success. And because of the racial animosity that has resulted from the constant barrage of racism charges, many blacks instinctively oppose anything characterized as white. Consequently, African American students often automatically reject any behavior linked with "acting white," including speaking standard English, listening to classical music, studying at the library, receiving academic awards, going to museums, doing volunteer work, being on time, and reading poetry.[43] Teacher Marc Elrich similarly reports that black students treat those who succeed in school as white "wannabes."[44] A black student who pursues scholarly achievement is "jumped after school for answering too many questions" in the classroom; as one assaulter said, "Dude, you're whiter than they [whites] are."[45] A sixteen-year-old Hispanic girl is accused of acting white because she excels in school. She gets teased for using "SAT words" when she's out with her friends. And these attitudes persist even as minority students climb the educational ladder. At college, black students who join traditionally white fraternities or sororities often face accusations from fellow blacks that they are self-hating sellouts.[46] Exemplifying the negative image acquired by minorities who assimilate into the majority culture, for instance, Supreme Court Justice Clarence Thomas is described by some African Americans as "the whitest man in America."[47]

In explaining the disappointing performance of black students in Shaker Heights, Ogbu characterizes as "dismal" the level of black parental involvement in the education of their children. His primary solution to the academic woes of black students is for the black community to take greater responsibility for the education of its children. This approach is similarly endorsed by comedian Bill Cosby, who says that blacks need to become more active in regulating their young people's behavior. In Cosby's view, blacks concentrate so much on racism that they ignore the culture in which their children are raised. The reality of this culture is graphically depicted in Jewelle Taylor Gibbs's description of an African American underclass where youths "sell drugs openly on major thoroughfares without fear of apprehension, teenage girls have multiple out-of-wedlock pregnancies without fear of ostracism, youthful gangs terrorize neighborhoods without fear of retaliation, and young teenagers loiter aimlessly at night on street corners without fear of reprobation."[48]

Thomas Sowell likewise argues that culture is to blame for many of the problems experienced by African Americans.[49] As evidence contradicting the claim that racism is responsible for the dilemmas of African Americans, Sowell points to a Harvard University study indicating that most of its black alumni are from either the East Indies or Africa or were the children of West Indian or African immigrants. These alumni are of the same race as African Americans, and yet they experience a rate of success unmatched by African Americans. According to Sowell, "The counterproductive and self-destructive culture of blacks . . . in today's ghettos is regarded by many as the only authentic black culture."[50]

A medium-sized company had just settled a racial discrimination suit. One piece of evidence that hurt its case was its relatively small percentage of minority employees. Consequently, its human resources director instituted a program aimed at attracting and retaining minority employees. Under this program, every minority employee would be assigned a senior mentor who would provide assistance and support. In addition, any disciplinary action involving a minority employee was to be reviewed by a cultural sensitivity officer in the personnel office.

Three years later, the company was served with another racial discrimination suit, which alleged in part that minority employees had been stigmatized.

The ubiquitous allegations of racism provide a convenient excuse for disregarding any deeper causes. As the Reverend Al Sharpton has said, "We must not reprimand our children" for violent or antisocial behavior, because that violence and antisocialism "was put in them by an oppressive system."[51] But contradictions arise when blacks naturally reject being described as individuals who cannot shape their own destiny and yet attribute all their failings to the outside dictates of social racism. Similar contradictions exist when prominent upper-class blacks identify themselves with the most criminally prone, antisocial, unemployed, lower-class urban youth. Despite the fact that the black middle class has tripled in size since 1968, members of that class act as if they are still confined to ghettoes. Thus the image of the violent and rebellious black youth serves as the cultural model even for upper-class blacks. As Debra Dickerson states in *The End of Blackness*, the black community "needs to unravel the mystery of why its most successful act like the most dispossessed." And according to Dinesh D'Souza:

> Middle-class behavior by African-Americans is seen as inauthentic, while low-class behavior is seen as genuinely black. . . . Thus, while most immigrant groups tend to look to their most successful citizens for emulation

and self-definition, on many issues the moral tone in the black community is set from below.[52]

The black underclass achieves such an influential role, D'Souza argues, because it is perceived as the most oppositional and resistant to white middle-class standards. For this reason, instead of trying to counter the cultural and moral influence of rap's raw and decrepit lyrics, the leaders of the African American community often celebrate rap music as the expression of black authenticity.

Sociologists describe the ghetto-style culture of the black underclass as the "cool-pose culture."[53] Not only is this culture immensely fulfilling to underclass blacks, because it glorifies defiance of social authority, but it also tends to bring them much respect from envious white youths. Indeed, this may explain "the otherwise puzzling finding by social psychologists that young black men and women tend to have the highest levels of self-esteem of all ethnic groups, and that their self-image is independent of how badly they were doing in school."[54] Not surprisingly, this "cool-pose culture" and adulation of underclass rebellion is being adopted by new immigrants. According to Cesar Barrios, an outreach worker for a social services agency in New York City, Mexican Americans who encounter hardship and difficulties in their new home are quickly lured to the black underclass culture and its rebellious rejection of conventional norms. Consequently, young Mexicans "prefer to imitate blacks [rather] than white people," Barrios notes.[55]

Criticizing the black embracement of underclass norms, Stanley Crouch in *The Artificial White Man: Essays on Authenticity* expresses disgust for the tasteless vulgarity of black rap music. He argues that if white producers had sponsored such "music," they would have been "run off the planet." Crouch laments the cultural elevation of urban street mores and worries about how a struggling black population will handle the "redefinition of black authenticity all the way downward." In particular, Crouch bemoans the hero-worship of ill-behaved professional basketball players and the "present disengagement" of the black community from the world of education.

CONTRARY TO all the racism allegations, African Americans have made significant progress. While the median income of white households rose 19 percent between 1980 and 2000, that of black families rose 39 percent. From 1970 to 2000, the most dramatic gains in life expectancy occurred in black men.[56] During the same time period, the percentage of blacks earning a high school diploma increased from 31 percent to 79 percent, and the proportion of blacks with college degrees quadrupled. From 1980 to 2000, the number of black households with annual incomes exceeding seventy-five thousand dollars increased more than 150 percent. During the ten-year period from 1992 to 2002, the poverty rate for blacks fell almost a third. Currently, the median income of black women is about 90 percent that of white women. And in the political arena, the number of black elected officials grew during the twenty years following 1972 from a couple of hundred to well over six thousand.[57]

The opportunities available to blacks in America are reflected in the career evolution of rapper Snoop Doggy Dogg. The one-time gang leader and convict has gone from making gangsta rap and porn videos to producing video games and MTV specials, appearing in major motion pictures, writing a best-selling autobiography, starring in a family-oriented feature film (*Coach Snoop*), and even marketing a popular doll modeled after himself. As Michelle Malkin notes, "Only in America could a cop-hating former crack dealer transmogrify into an intergenerational plastic toy (complete with 'Doggystyle' clothes)."[58]

Pervasive charges of racism, however, often mask any evidence contradicting that racism. For instance, even though employment discrimination and other civil rights cases now represent a third of all federal civil trials, almost half of all jury verdicts in favor of plaintiffs are reversed by the appellate courts,[59] with only 6 percent of employers' victories being reversed.[60] Yet despite the fact that appeals courts frequently find verdicts in discrimination cases to be unsupported by the law, there continues to be a boom in such lawsuit filings, which increased nearly threefold from 1990 to 2000.[61] This boom has occurred even though, when employment discrimination complaints actually get a hearing, it frequently turns out that the complainants were not hired because they had poor job qualifications.[62] Further contradicting the claim that racism is pervasive in the workplace is a Hudson Institute survey indicating that more than 50 percent of the corporations studied had instituted diversity training, mentoring, and promotion programs. Still another survey shows that diversity-related initiatives covered nearly three-quarters of the American workforce.[63]

The unprecedented economic expansion of the 1990s achieved precisely what experts predicted would lift black males out of their poverty and marginalization. Millions of new jobs were created; the unemployment rate sank to all-time lows; help-wanted signs appeared everywhere. But African American men did not take these jobs; instead, the jobs were filled by African American women and by immigrant men, including Hispanics from Latin America and blacks from the Caribbean. Recent studies have shown that economic growth has brought gains to black women and other racial and ethnic groups, but not to African American men, who are becoming increasingly disconnected from mainstream society.[64] "There's something very different happening with young black men, and it's something we can no longer ignore," says Ronald B. Mincy, professor of social work at Columbia University.[65]

One of the most common objects of racial discrimination charges in the employment arena has been police departments. But again, significant evidence contradicts those charges. For every position in the New York City Police Department for which promotion is discretionary (and hence not determined by an objective merit test), blacks and Hispanics become detectives almost five years earlier than whites. Moreover, whites wait twice as long to be appointed to high-ranking positions, such as deputy inspector or deputy chief, than do blacks and Hispanics.[66]

THE POWER of racism accusations to completely stifle or dismiss any other explanation is illustrated by a February 2005 60 *Minutes* story on the adoption of black American children by white Canadian parents. The story implied that American racism was to blame for the relative infrequency of "transracial" adoptions in the United States. But what the story ignored was the fact that the National Association of Black Social Workers had for decades decried transracial adoptions in the United States as "cultural genocide."[67] The story also ignored the fact that white families, discouraged from adopting black American babies, have turned to countries like Korea and China to adopt Asian babies.

Health is another area in which racism allegations tend to repress any other issue or explanation. Studies show, for instance, that black men are twice as likely to die of prostrate cancer than are white men. Yet while this racial disparity is often attributed to some form of racism, other studies show that black men are less likely to seek blood tests that would detect the disease.[68] At the other end of the age spectrum, black children are often shown to do less well in school than white children. This too is blamed on racism. Yet studies show that black children are less likely to get sufficient sleep than are their white counterparts, making them more susceptible to poorer school performance.[69]

He was the commencement speaker at the college's graduation exercises. He was a well-known entertainer; his limousine was parked outside the auditorium; he wore a fifteen-thousand-dollar suit. But his speech wasn't about his successes.

"We are locked into inner-city cesspools," he told the crowd.

"Oftentimes, crime is the only route available to us," he said.

"Wherever we go, we're looked on as pimps and drug dealers."

"The schools to which we send our kids are like prisons."

And the mostly white crowd, whose Chevrolets and Hondas filled the parking lot outside, just nodded.

At a reception following the speech, the entertainer was approached by one of the college administrators.

"It was a very enlightening speech," he said. "I had no idea, but it must be awful where you live. How bad is the crime, really?"

"What! You automatically presume I live in the ghetto? Just because I'm black?"

The media has played a prime role in creating and sustaining many of the confusions and inconsistencies in racial matters. Instead of dedicating itself to exposing the truth in whatever form it may come, the media has been swept up in perpetuating a kind of politically correct double standard.

Minority journalists criticize the media for overstating the degree of criminal behavior among minorities. Yet as William McGowan reveals in *Coloring the News*, the media often refuse to disclose any facts suggesting criminal culpability of minorities arrested by the police.[70] In *Volunteer Slavery*, journalist Jill Nelson writes that blacks serve as "pathological, scatological slices of life waiting to be chewed, digested and excreted into the requisite number of column inches in the paper." And yet many media outlets deliberately refuse to publicize negative information about minorities. In 1995 the *New York Times Magazine* published a glowing profile on Patrick Chavis, a black physician who had become a symbol for the success of affirmative action. But not long after the article appeared, Chavis was barred from practicing medicine. Not only did he have a shocking record of malfeasance, but evidence of that malfeasance existed long before the *New York Times Magazine* article was written.

The media also tends not to provide information that corrects or contradicts previous accusations of racism. When swastikas were painted on the doors of black soldiers at Fort Bragg, blame was immediately placed on racist white soldiers. The story received national attention, and Fort Bragg was painted as a hotbed of racism. Yet two months later, when a black soldier was found to be the culprit, the media paid no attention.

Likewise, when a black minister in Texas blamed two church fires on "pervasive racism," *ABC News Tonight* made it a lead story. But later, when an eighteen-year-old black man was indicted for both fires, the story received only scant mention late in the newscast. And even after several studies had shown that a series of black church fires in the South in the 1990s was not the result of a racial conspiracy, the *New York Times* published an article asserting that the fires reflected the racism of the old South.

On matters of race, the media often ignores the full story. The *Los Angeles Times* has obscured the links between drug production and illegal immigration, and the *New York Times* has been reluctant to acknowledge immigration as a factor in school overcrowding.[71] When a black Pennsylvania man killed three people and wounded two, all white, the *New York Times* did not report any details of the man's history of racism, including his shouting: "I'm not gonna kill any black people; I'm gonna kill all white people."[72] Nor did the *Times* disclose that a gang of black teenage muggers had admitted vowing to confine their attacks to whites, or that in other instances, black assailants were heard to call their victims "white bitch" and "white ho" and "white KKK bitch."[73] At Gannett newspapers, corporate policies have required a certain number of pictures of minorities in each paper, regardless of news value.[74] But a racial-quota policy at a Gannett-owned newspaper in Vermont, requiring that one-sixth of the subjects in a photo series called "Vermont Voices" be a "person of color," had to be discontinued when the scarcity of nonwhites in the community meant that the same faces of color appeared over and over. Another policy required the newspaper's columnist to devote one out of every four columns to minority issues.

In its attempt to accommodate a certain racial image, the media sometimes takes rather extreme measures. When reporting news of crimes and giving descriptions of suspects, for instance, many newspapers deliberately omit the detail of race, even when those suspects are considered dangerous and still at large. Another example of racial or cultural sensitivities completely suffocating objective news coverage can be found in the way the *New York Times* and National Public Radio covered the practice of arranged marriages among immigrants from South Asia. Although these media outlets would normally be highly critical of such a custom if perpetuated in any other setting, both treated the custom with deference bordering on admiration when practiced by racial minorities.[75] But perhaps the *Sacramento Bee* exhibited the most extreme sensitivities in what it called "An Apology to Our Readers:"

> On page A-1, we ran what was initially seen as a cute, innocent picture of two children dressing up for Halloween. But what was not caught in the editing process was the stereotype enforced in the picture of an African-American child dressed in a maid's uniform putting lipstick on a child dressed in a party outfit. The implication of the images in the picture and the words in the headline should have been recognized and they should not have run. We were wrong, and our sincere apologies are offered. A hard lesson in the area of sensitivity has been learned.[76]

Racial portrayals in popular entertainment are similarly cautious. In a survey of more than six hundred television entertainment programs aired over three decades, researchers found that 90 percent of the murders were committed by whites, while only 3 percent were committed by blacks.[77] Thus, on television, blacks are about twenty times less likely to commit homicide than they are in real life. Yet despite this skewed portrayal, an author of a report on media bias states that although he would never say that *all* movies are racist, he has "yet to find one that isn't."[78]

Notwithstanding the well-known political correctness of Hollywood, accusations abound as to the discriminatory content in movies and television programs.[79] Even *The Cosby Show*, which portrayed blacks in a consistently positive light, has been criticized as catering to white racism, since it depicted the Huxtable family in a way that did not make whites face up to the evils they have inflicted on blacks. By not showing how the Huxtables were disadvantaged in a white world, *The Cosby*

Show is said to have relieved whites of the guilt they should feel.[80] But herein lies the paradox: if a show is racist for depicting blacks as criminals and outcasts, a show is also racist if it depicts blacks as successful career people in a well-adjusted family.

At a private reception preceding a theater opening, an investment banker who was a well-known social progressive criticized someone who was complaining about the work styles of certain employees. "We need to celebrate cultural uniqueness, not stifle it," he proclaimed. "We need to make the extra effort for diversity."

Earlier that day, the banker had fired a young black assistant for not being sufficiently deferential to an important client.

Although racial sensitivities may be more harsh and confusing to whites, the realities of life are often more harsh to blacks. But this harshness will never be truly addressed if it is clouded by contradiction and confusion. Racial justice cannot be achieved if the mere concept of racism is bogged down in conflicting dictates. Nor can race continue to operate in an ideological vacuum in which nothing else—neither culture nor the individual—has any contributing influence whenever something bad happens to a member of a racial minority. Can race be the sole explanation for why the percentage of black children living with both parents through the age of seventeen has dropped to 6 percent from 50 percent? With Asians excelling in education and Middle Easterners excelling in business, as just two examples among many, can blacks blame racism exclusively for any failures they experience in the classroom or the boardroom?

The civil rights leadership in the United States sometimes resembles the old Palestinian Liberation Organization in its single-minded, combative approach to race. That leadership came of political age during the street protests of the 1960s, and they are still fighting—always blaming racism, just as the PLO always blames Israel. But the battle over racism has largely been won; the challenge now is how to manage the peace.

FOUR

The Only Sin
in a CultuRe of
Moral RelativiSm

HE WAS not the leading politician in the state, nor was he even a prominent politician—at least, not until he was caught on film during his Caribbean vacation, smoking pot on the patio outside his cabana. Why the television station had sent someone to photograph him was never explained: the station manager was too busy defending himself against all the other attacks.

"What's the big deal?" a supporter of the politician inquired. "He was just on vacation. Nobody was getting hurt."

"Marijuana's really no different from alcohol, and what's a vacation without a few drinks?" someone else argued.

"Compared to all the bad things in the world, I don't see that this is any big deal."

"Show me someone who hasn't fudged the rules while on vacation, and I'll show you someone who's never taken a vacation."

By the time the story had run its course, the Federal Communications Commission had been asked to investigate possible violations of the television station's broadcast license. Meanwhile, having increased his name recognition, the politician was considering running for governor.

The term *moral relativism* is often used to describe the state of cultural values in contemporary America. This moral relativism took root in the 1960s during the sexual revolution's crusade against the cultural mores and behavioral codes of the past. In addition to the demise of traditional moral dictates, character traits that had been unquestioned for centuries also came under attack. Humility, reticence, and self-sacrifice were seen as unwanted remnants of an oppressive and intolerant culture.

The rise of the self-esteem movement in the 1990s constituted yet another assault on the legitimacy of traditional moral codes. Self-expression and self-fulfillment became the new guideposts of individual behavior. Moral rules were seen as injurious to the self. The notions of "sin" and "vice" were discredited as "unhealthy." Self-help gurus urged people to do "whatever makes you happy." There were no such things as moral problems, just psychological ones. Right and wrong were not absolutes; everything was relative; it was up to individuals to determine for themselves what was "appropriate."

Under this culture of self-gratification and moral relativism, American society has drifted into a psychology of grievance and entitlement. Whereas traditional virtues such as self-discipline, courage, and responsibility require self-denial, contemporary culture sees self-denial as antithetical to self-fulfillment—the pseudovirtue so pervasive in the modern age. And whereas traditional morality sought to elevate individuals to higher standards formulated outside the realm of the individual, the modern "culture of the self" makes individuals and all their selfish desires the center of all "moral" and behavioral rules.

Modern society has traded in moral people for economic and psychological people. Materialism has become the defining feature of the times, not just materialism in the property sense, but materialism in the moral sense. The issues that get characterized as moral issues are those associated with materialistic and physical well-being. Teen smoking is tightly regulated, but teen sex is largely ignored. It's a crime to put a child into a car without a proper car seat, but there's no moral taboo against exposing that child to sexually explicit lyrics or videos. Regular attendance at a health club is considered a high mark of individual well-being, but regular attendance at a church or synagogue is not. The current therapeutic culture mandates full and open self-disclosure of one's emotions, and yet one's religious beliefs are expected to be kept private. Political candidates' college grades can be analyzed, but not their moral beliefs. Vice is redefined as disease, and virtue is equated with intolerance. Pornography is free speech, yet opposition to affirmative action is hate. Prenatal health care is a moral issue, but abortion is not. Drug use and gang membership are social problems, not moral evils. Repression of one's emotions is wrong, and yet lying is . . . well, it depends.

Homecoming week at the university was the biggest social event of the year. It culminated in the football game on Saturday afternoon and a concert on Saturday night. This year, the concert featured one of the hottest music groups in the country. Tickets had been sold out for months. Hotel vacancies were nonexistent in the medium-sized city in which the university was situated. It was the biggest thing that had happened in the city in years.

On the afternoon of the concert, the lead singer of the group was arrested at the airport on a drug charge. A fairly small amount had been found on the singer, but the police were keeping him in custody—something about resisting arrest.

The concert had to be canceled. The students were furious. The university was indignant. Within the week, the police chief was fired.

Just as in the market economy, where the consumer is always right, so too in a culture of moral relativism is the individual the sole authority. But this individualism is not defined in terms of civic duties and moral responsibilities. As David Frum argues, modern society has mutated into "a society that is engulfed in its own feelings and . . . that gives priority to the self over the community."[1]

Even corporate culture has adopted the attitudes of the 1960s counterculture. Just listen to the advertisements. "The world has boundaries, ignore them," proclaims a car ad while one of its vehicles crashes into a huge sign that says "Rules." An eyewear company uses the refrain "no limits." A brokerage firm "knows no boundaries." A restaurant chain says, "Sometimes you gotta break the rules." Another says, "No rules, just right." A department store: "No rules here." An entertainment retailer: "We broke the rules." Though "Just do it!" was once a call for sexual freedom, it is now an athletic shoe slogan. Whereas in the 1960s hippies and draft-card burners preached rebellion, today's rebellion is being sold on prime-time television.

In *The Rise of Selfishness in America*, James Lincoln Collier attributes many of the nation's social ills to the demise of the Victorian value system and its replacement by a culture of the self.[2] James Q. Wilson argues that American society is morally confused, reluctant to make any judgments about what is right or wrong.[3] In *The Fourth Great Awakening and the Future of Egalitarianism*, Nobel laureate Robert William Fogel observes that modern society has made great progress in every area save one—the promotion of moral behavior. According to Fogel, in a society prone to teenage pregnancy, drug addiction, and crime, moral values are more important than mere cash in lifting up the poor.

Historian Gertrude Himmelfarb argues that the nation's problem is not that it has the wrong morality but that it has no morality at all.[4] Because of moral relativism, which urges people to be nonjudgmental, American society is left with no standards other than codified law to govern sex, marriage, divorce, children, and crime.[5] Having devalued the middle-class virtues of social order, self-discipline, and individual restraint, America has experienced soaring rates of sexual harassment, divorce, domestic abuse, social rage, and cultural division. For instance, the removal of cultural and moral stigma against out-of-wedlock births resulted in a 419 percent increase in illegitimate births during the three decades following 1960.[6] Over the same time period, violent crime increased 560 percent and divorce rates quadrupled.

Coinciding with the rise of moral relativism has been a decline in the exercise of moral judgment. This deterioration was especially evident during Bill Clinton's presidency. With each revelation of each new moral scandal, the country was urged to just "move on" to the "other issues" of more pressing concern, like Social Security reform. Moral judgment is messy, time-consuming, and distracting, the message went. It is also outdated, intolerant, and oppressive, because if all people are to determine for themselves what is moral, then no one has a right to impose a moral judgment on them. But America's moral indifference toward the Clinton presidency marked a sharp departure from the recent past. During the presidential campaign of 1988, for instance, revelations of plagiarism forced Joseph Biden out of the race.

The lowering of cultural standards reflects a sort of resigned contentment to match expectations with an ever-declining reality—a reality in which people celebrate sports championships by burning and pillaging their own cities.[7] During much of the past century, for instance, the debate over the well-being of youth covered a broad social terrain, as Barbara Dafoe Whitehead observes in her study on contemporary sex education.[8] The deliberations of the decennial White House Conference on Children, which began in 1909 and ended in the early 1970s, ranged from improving health and schooling to building character and citizenship. Today, however, public ambitions for adolescent well-being are much narrower. Debate on the nation's youth has come down to a few questions. How do we keep boys from killing people? How do we keep girls from having babies? How do we limit the social havoc caused by adolescent acting-out? This culturally lowered, valueless mentality puts blame on the police every time an intoxicated mob vandalizes buildings and assaults innocent passersby. It's a mentality that has allowed college graduates to have worse reading and writing skills than the graduates of thirty years ago.[9] Indeed, at many campuses of the California State University system, almost 40 percent of the courses taken by first-year students are remedial courses aimed at teaching elementary reading, writing, and arithmetic.[10]

Marie was a tenth-grade social sciences teacher in the second-largest public high school in the city. Her classroom was on the second floor in the northwest corner of the building. She used to take the small, enclosed stairway just outside of her classroom whenever she wanted to go to the faculty lounge. But she doesn't anymore, not since she ran into that couple laid out on the steps.

She had walked right past them, trying to pretend not to notice, even as she had to swerve to avoid them. Such things were supposed to be against school regulations, but Marie didn't want to get a reputation for being a prude. Besides, who was she to judge?

The degree to which hesitancy to exercise moral judgment has taken hold can be seen in the social backlash against those institutions that actually take strong moral positions. The Catholic Church, for instance, has been vilified for its stands on abortion and gay marriage. When the Vatican advised U.S. bishops on the administering of Communion to Catholic politicians who support abortion rights, the church became the target of slurs by those claiming that the church should not inject its moral beliefs on society. Even a nondenominational youth-development institution like the Boy Scouts has come under attack for its moral views. Because of the organization's stand against homosexuality, a group of young scouts who appeared on stage at the 2000 Democratic convention to lead the Pledge of Allegiance was booed. Despite a recognized First Amendment right to keep avowed gays from being Scout leaders, numerous cities and school districts have withdrawn their sponsorship of the Boy Scouts. At other times and with other issues, however, a near complete indifference is shown to those who strive to be society's moral leaders. When Jesse Jackson, a self-proclaimed voice of America's "moral conscience" and a spiritual adviser to President Clinton, was discovered to be making secret payments from his nonprofit corporation to support an out-of-wedlock child by his mistress, there was virtually no moral criticism from the mainstream media or political officials.[11]

Just as a culture of moral relativism condemned Vice President Dan Quayle for his criticism of the way Hollywood glamorized single parenthood, so too does it forbid the categorization of any non-Western culture as defective or destructive in any way. Even after the horrors of terrorism were revealed by the attacks of 9/11, there was still an outrage when President Bush described certain terrorist states as forming an "axis of evil." Indeed, relativists teach that all cultures and societies—whether the Taliban or Saddam Hussein's Baathists—are qualitatively no worse or better than any other society or culture.[12] Under moral relativism, there is a hesitancy to describe anything as "bad" or "evil," except for Adolf Hitler, who seems to be the only surviving link that the present world has with evil.

She was the youngest principal to ever serve at Lincoln High. The students seemed to love her. She had energy and a doctoral degree from a top-tier university. She was also having a fairly well-known affair with a married coach at a nearby school. And her picture was in the newspaper after the police raided an alternative club she frequented. There were a few parents who called on the school board to investigate, but they were widely criticized as moralistic inquisitors, intolerant of diversity.

There is one exception to America's moral relativism—race. Regarding charges of racial discrimination, there is no taboo on judgmentalism. No permissive, laissez faire attitude. No "whatever feels right to you" approach. The one sin in America against which every teacher, every politician, and every corporate marketing department can preach is racial discrimination. And, indeed, it is a sin deserving of universal condemnation. But what is noteworthy about the current moral climate is that racial discrimination is the *only* such sin.

The nation's schools have been cleansed of any moral perspective. Children are instructed on all the various forms of domestic arrangements that qualify as "families." They are taught safe-sex methods, including masturbation and how to use condoms. They are told that prostitution is a lifestyle choice. But never, in absolutely no circumstances, can they allow themselves to even passively acquiesce in an act of racial discrimination. They cannot draw pictures of Judeo-Christian religious symbols, but they can recreate the religious rituals of African tribes. Maryland elementary students cannot recite Pilgrim prayers, even at Thanksgiving, but schools in Michigan can broadcast Islamic prayers over public loudspeakers several times a day.[13]

Not only is racial discrimination the only unquestioned moral wrong in America, it is the only wrong that carries an automatic presumption of guilt. When accusations of racism are made, it is up to the accused to prove his or her innocence. A denial is not enough; indeed, whites are seen to have little trustworthiness on any matter of race, and there is little they can do to defend themselves once an accusation is levied. It is even doubtful whether any accusation of racism, no matter how unfounded, can ever be discredited completely. This is because any hint or possibility of racism, no matter how undefined or speculative, is enough to leave a perpetual curtain of guilt hanging over the accused.

As the primary social sin, race trumps everything else. It overshadows all other concerns. Race can even supersede obedience to the law, as exemplified by those universities and law schools that for years brazenly operated illegal quota systems in their admissions of minority students.[14] Race renders irrelevant any other consideration, as exemplified in cases where police are accused of racism whenever they arrest a racial minority. In those cases, a strictly one-way focus is adopted: whereas police conduct is minutely examined, the conduct of the suspect leading up to the arrest is rarely scrutinized. In June 2004, for instance, the Los Angeles Police were accused of beating a suspect whom they had just apprehended after a high-speed car chase and foot pursuit.[15] The incident revived memories of the Rodney King incident, with the police being accused of racism. Never raised, however, was the issue of whether it is at all reasonable for an auto-theft suspect—after leading the police on a high-speed car chase through miles of city streets, then sprinting from his car once he had crashed it, and throwing up his arms in surrender only after being surrounded by squads of police—to expect police officers who have rightly feared for their own safety to suddenly treat the suspect as if he were no more dangerous than a jay-walking dowager. A similar rush to accuse the police occurred when an officer fatally shot a thirteen-year-old auto thief who had tried to run him over after a car chase had come to an end. Immediately after the incident, before any investigation had even commenced, a leader of the black community proclaimed: "I wouldn't doubt it if that officer said, 'I'm gonna kill this n[—].'"[16] But not all black leaders blame the police for urban violence. Ted Hayes, a social activist, instead faults "the lackadaisical inner-city family culture" implicitly supported by black church leaders.[17]

The issue is not whether racism deserves to be treated as a serious wrong but whether it deserves to crowd out every other wrong. Everyone remembers Mark Fuhrman, the investigator accused of racism in the O. J. Simpson trial, but who remembers the names of the executives of World-Com who perpetuated the largest corporate fraud in history? Most people associate the Denny's restaurant chain with the racial discrimination suit brought against it, but do as many people remember the $340 million criminal fine—up to that time the largest criminal fine ever imposed in the United States—paid by Daiwa Bank in 1996 for defrauding bank regulators? Or the $500 million fine levied on F. Hoffmann-LaRoche Ltd. in 1999 for leading a worldwide conspiracy to fix vitamin prices in the United States? Or the criminal penalties imposed on Summitville Consolidated Mining Co. for poisoning a water supply with cyanide, causing a sixteen-mile stretch of the Alamosa River to become biologically dead?

A 2006 scandal involving the Duke University lacrosse team exemplifies how race often overshadows all other moral concerns. In that scandal, three white Duke players were accused of sexually assaulting a black woman who had been hired to strip at a party attended by the players. The incident became national news. Even though Duke immediately canceled the remainder of its lacrosse season, critics claimed that the university was not taking the scandal seriously.[18] For days and weeks afterward, the incident stayed in the media spotlight. The university came under attack from all directions, including faculty, students, and alumni. In a full-page ad in the college newspaper, the department of African and African American Studies along with other departments called the situation a "social disaster." However, the attacks on the university seemed strangely different from the reactions to other sexual assaults committed by college athletes. Unfortunately, sexual assaults by male athletes have become an all-too-common occurrence, and the rise of sexual violence poses an extremely serious danger to society. But the controversy and debate surrounding the Duke incident virtually ignored this heinous act of violence. Instead, it focused almost exclusively on the racial aspect of the incident—the allegation that the white players had assaulted a black victim. This racial focus also ignored the broader moral setting of the incident. In an e-mail message sent less than two hours after the alleged rape, one of the lacrosse players said that he wanted to invite the strippers to his room, kill them, and cut off their skin. Clearly, anyone who would send such a message had already crossed the boundary of acceptable behavior, had already been morally corrupted by a nihilistic, anything-goes culture. In fact, during the three years preceding the incident, Duke lacrosse players had received fifteen notices of violations for crass misconduct. But this culture of immoral and destructive behavior was lost amid the singular focus on the racial aspect of the incident.

The power of race to diminish or mitigate even the most depraved behavior was revealed in the case of Colin Ferguson, the man who killed six people during a shooting rampage on the Long Island Railroad in December 1993. When Ferguson blamed his actions on "black rage"—anger over racism in America—almost half the people surveyed in a public poll agreed that this defense was legitimate.[19] Thus, an ambiguous allegation of racism was powerful enough to turn the perpetrator of a shocking crime into a victim. A Hmong man used this strategy after he was arrested for shooting and killing six Wisconsin hunters in November 2004; he justified the murders by claiming that the hunters had shouted racial epithets at him. And on a less tragic level, minorities staging fake burglaries or vandalism for insurance purposes have spray-painted racial slurs on their own property in order to deflect suspicion from themselves as well as to elicit unconditional sympathy.[20]

Jason had moved to a new neighborhood. He found a job at a data processing company about a mile from his new home. The presidential campaign was on the news every night, and Jason saw the political signs every day on his way to work.

On election day, a co-worker invited him to go with her to vote after work. The polling place, however, had no record of Jason's name. He had never registered, he said. Then they asked for a photo I.D., but he had none. They said if he could produce a piece of mail addressed to him, he could still register. The polls were open for another hour, they said.

On his way out the door, he was approached by a lawyer who wanted to take down his name for a voter-discrimination lawsuit.

Every four years the country is reminded by celebrities through public-service advertisements that voting is one of the most important duties and privileges possessed by a free people. Voting is the pillar of democracy, the messages proclaim. And the fact that it is an activity performed relatively infrequently—for most people, once every four years—only heightens its importance.

None of the celebrities in their public-service messages would equate voting with such mundane, everyday activities as, say, driving a car. And yet there is the expectation that voting is something that should require very little effort or advance planning. To obtain a driver's license, one must pass a written exam and then a road test; one must submit all the correct forms in a timely fashion and to the correct governmental office; one must provide all the requested information and pay the mandated fee. If any of these requirements are not met, the license is denied. However, when it comes to issues involving minority voting, little consideration is given to the individual's duty to perform a few minimal requirements. If minority voters fail to register to vote and then are denied the right to cast a ballot on election day, this denial is given a purely racial interpretation. If a minority voter appears at the wrong polling place and is denied a ballot, racism is blamed. If a minority voter shows up late to a polling place and is denied entrance, this denial is seen as racial disenfranchisement.

As the primary (if not exclusive) social sin, racism negates all other sins. The fact that a criminal defendant has been dealing drugs is not as heinous as the possibility that the arresting officer or prosecutor harbored racist attitudes. The fact that a suspect carried a gun and resisted arrest is not as important as the statistically disproportionate number of blacks arrested. When a corporation settles a racial-discrimination suit, it frequently agrees to hold a series of diversity training seminars. But when a corporation settles a fraud suit, there is rarely any demand that the corporation host a series of ethics seminars. When new teachers are hired for public school positions, they undergo lengthy diversity-counseling sessions, but they receive very little training on actual classroom-management techniques.[21] When the *Boston Globe*'s first black female columnist was fired for fabricating quotes and making up fictitious characters, the editor of the paper confessed that he had harbored strong suspicions for years of the fabricating but had done nothing because he did not want to be seen as singling out a black woman.[22]

Yet despite its being the primary social sin, racism is a largely undefined wrong with no clear boundaries. For instance, a school board chairperson's spontaneous description of an angry group of minority parents as a "lynch mob" was denounced as "race-baiting and racial harassment at its worst."[23] Even English-only rules in the workplace have been seen as discriminatory, as evidenced by a 612 percent increase in such claims from 1996 to 2002.[24] This lack of certainty regarding what constitutes racism has created a moral and social anxiety. A fear of somehow reinforcing some hidden stereotype or violating some unknown racial rule leads to a fear of expressing any kind of moral judgment. This is particularly evident in the nation's reluctance to take any action on the massive illegal immigration coming in through America's southern border. Politicians and government officials are so afraid of being accused of racial discrimination, they are hesitant to even discuss the transformative social changes occurring as a result of illegal immigration. This climate of fear allowed California's passage of Proposition 187, which denied taxpayer-funded services such as free education and free hospital treatment to illegal aliens, to be characterized as "one of the darkest moments in America's long history of racism towards people of color."[25] Even after the terrorist attacks of September 11, 2001, eleven states continued to issue driver's licenses to illegal aliens. This practice continued despite the fact that three of the nineteen 9/11 hijackers had been stopped in the months preceding the attacks, but none had not been arrested because they possessed valid driver's licenses. And almost all of the 9/11 hijackers had used their driver's licenses to board the planes that fateful day.[26]

The racial attack on a Waller County, Texas, district attorney reflects the way in which racism charges can hinder or block the enforcement of valid and necessary laws. The district attorney had circulated a legal opinion in which he stated that he would prosecute any Prairie View A&M University students who attempted to vote illegally in upcoming elections. According to the district attorney, students in the past had "feigned residency and deprived Waller Countians of fair elections."[27] Although Waller County was mostly white, the majority of its black population were students attending Prairie View A&M. Consequently, the NAACP complained to the Texas attorney general, alleging that the

Waller County district attorney was pursuing a racist agenda. Further "evidence" of the district attorney's racism came from the fact that he had previously indicted the black mayor of Brookshire, Texas, for assaulting and injuring an elderly person.

Perhaps the best illustration of how race overshadows everything else, even life-and-death concerns, can be seen in the government's discrimination case against American Airlines—a case that reveals the national paralysis caused by the country's racial politics. Alleging discrimination in the treatment of certain passengers after 9/11, the Transportation Department sued American Airlines and United, Delta, and Continental. According to the government's complaint, the refusal of American Airlines to allow ten people (out of twenty-three million passengers) board its planes in the last four months of 2001 constituted illegal discrimination. Typical of those ten was a man named Jehad Alshrafi. After being informed by a federal air marshal that Alshrafi's name resembled one on a terror watch list and that Alshrafi had been acting suspiciously at the gate, an American Airlines pilot refused to let Alshrafi board a November 3, 2001, flight out of Boston. But as alleged in the subsequent lawsuit, the only reason Alshrafi was denied boarding was because of racial or national-origin discrimination, even though there were at least five other passengers of Arab descent who had been allowed to board.[28]

The four airlines all settled, paying millions of dollars into a fund that would be spent on "sensitivity training." The airlines settled even though they have a responsibility for protecting tens of millions of people in the wake of the worst terrorist attack in history, even though the government had warned of an imminent terror attack and told the airlines to be particularly vigilant on three different occasions between 9/11 and the end of 2001, even though—in the words of the 9/11 Commission—this vigilance was supposed to be directed against "Islamic terrorism," and even though a fairly obvious requirement for being an Islamic terrorist is an Islamic identity.

After the university team won a championship game, the students flooded out of the bars and started rioting in the streets. Store windows were smashed, cars were overturned, fires were set, and dozens of injuries were caused. But in the aftermath of this melee, university officials could only blame the police for letting the riot get out of hand; there was no fault placed on the students. Even though the rioters were mostly white, a sizable contingent of black students was involved, and the university was already facing heated criticism about high dropout rates among black students.

In many ways, the issue of racism no longer resonates within the larger moral arena envisioned by Martin Luther King Jr., who relied on such sources as the Bible for his moral case against segregation. Instead, racial issues today simply reverberate within a shell of haphazard and ever-changing rules, which in turn have stemmed from an unprioritized dictatorship of antidiscrimination concerns. Such rules have resulted in a holding by New Jersey's Division on Civil Rights that nightclubs offering drink discounts on "ladies' nights" amounts to an unlawful form of discrimination.[29] They have also mandated that a black radio announcer be forced to publicly apologize for simply drawing an off-the-cuff analogy between the football replay in NFL games to video replays of the infamous Rodney King beating.[30]

The racial rules that now define social morality have failed to produce a more moral or ethical society. Consider, for instance, all the cheating scandals that have filled the news: the Enron, Adelphi, Tyco, and WorldCom frauds, the Jack Abramoff lobbying violations, and the MLB steroid scandal. Most likely, all the participants in these scandals believed intensely in the values of diversity and racial tolerance, and yet this belief did not translate into any moral or ethical behavior. Furthermore, according to John McWhorter in *Winning the Race: Beyond the Crisis in Black America*, all the politically correct racial politics and rules have not been able to uplift the conditions of blacks. In fact, the moral relativism spawned during the 1960s has damaged African Americans more than racism ever has. McWhorter argues that even though blacks faced more discrimination during the Jim Crow era of the late nineteenth and early twentieth centuries, their culture was healthier, with a stronger work ethic and less crime and illegitimacy. But during the 1960s, blacks were told to rebel against the moral and cultural values of the larger society. Consequently, although two out of ten blacks were born out of wedlock in 1960, the figure jumped to seven out of ten by the mid-1990s.

Instead of clear moral principles shaping the racial attitudes of the majority culture, white guilt has become the guiding factor. As Shelby Steele notes, "White guilt is best understood as a vacuum of moral authority," where whites "feel no authority to speak or judge and where they sense a great risk of being seen as racist."[31] But this guilt can have a morally corrosive effect on the authority of social institutions, which end up "deferring to the greater moral authority of minorities by lowering standards and remaining mute to minority mediocrity," all in an effort "to save the institution from the racist label."[32] Racial guilt also shows up in the opposition to the war in Iraq, where the critics are so worried about America's appearing to be a racist country attacking Arab Muslims that they cannot even think about the underlying justifications or reasons for the war.

Even when whites feel blameless, Steele argues, they defer to blacks on any moral question that involves race, "retreating in sober self-reflection if not outright apology."[33] As New Yorker writer Jeffrey Toobin observes, "There is a fear of being called racist that has a tremendous effect on people."[34] It is like a cult of grief in which whites are motivated only by a desire to somehow participate in the victimization process.

Driven not so much by any overarching moral imperative as by an instinctive urge to avoid guilt, whites are attracted to racial policies promising the appearance of redemption, even if those policies offer no real substantive benefit to racial minorities.[35] This preoccupation with guilt and with reviving a sense of racial innocence, according to Steele, is nowhere more evident than in America's universities:

At some of America's most elite universities, administrators have granted concessions in response to black student demands that all but sanction racial separatism on campus—black "theme" dorms, black students unions, black yearbooks, homecoming dances, and so on. I don't believe administrators sincerely believe in these separatist concessions. Most of them are liberals who see racial separatism as wrong. But black student demands pull them into the paradigm of self-preoccupied white guilt whereby they seek a quick redemption by offering special entitlements that go beyond fairness. In this, black students become invisible to them. Though blacks have the lowest grade point average of any group in American universities, administrators never sit down with them and "demand" in kind that they bring their grades up to par. The paradigm of white guilt makes the real problems of black students secondary to the need for white redemption. It also cuts these administrators off from their own values, which would most certainly discourage racial separatism and encourage higher black performance. Lastly, it makes for escapist policies. . . . What demonstrates more than anything the degree to which university administrators (and faculties) have been subdued by this paradigm is their refusal to lead black students, to tell them what they honestly think, to insist that they perform at a higher level, and to ask them to integrate themselves fully into campus life.[36]

Because of their guilt, Steele argues, whites "excuse failure in the black communities."[37] This was highlighted in the aftermath of Hurricane Katrina. Despite the incompetence of the black mayor in instigating relief efforts, despite the fact that black leadership for decades had been failing the residents of New Orleans—with a 58 percent dropout rate among the city's high school students, the highest homicide rate in the country, and rampant corruption in the city's police force—all the blame for the city's posthurricane woes were put on the whites in charge of the federal government. And because of racial guilt, President Bush in turn decided to dump billions of dollars of aid into the Crescent City.[38]

A pervasive yet undefined guilt, which accompanies pervasive yet undefined charges of racism, has imposed upon the majority culture a feeling of helplessness, which then further reinforces a moral retreat. But guilt and the shallow desire for the mere appearance of innocence are no substitutes for morality. They are also no substitutes for truth and reality, as shown by the white liberal response to problems raised about a federally funded antigang program in Milwaukee. Even though the black sheriff of Milwaukee County voiced grave concerns about the program, and even though the program could not account for the public funds it had received in the past, it was nonetheless renewed by "a liberal elite" who was "more than happy to look the other way" so as to keep up the appearance of racial correctness.[39] A similar "image" approach is used by white liberals who go to great lengths to portray blacks favorably in television ads and sitcoms, but who ignore the tough moral choices needed to confront the realities of minority life in America.

As Bernard Goldberg writes in *Arrogance: Rescuing America from the Media Elite*, there are "few forces on earth more powerful than white liberal guilt."[40] Even though many white liberals may suspect they are wrong in their racial policies, they continue to accuse as racist anyone holding contrary views—the reason being, Goldberg asserts, that they wish to "bask in their own moral superiority." In a revealing anecdote, Goldberg describes preparing to do a story on juveniles terrorizing a neighborhood in Orlando. Before traveling to Florida, his producer asked him if the juveniles were black or white. When he said he didn't know, she answered, "They need to be white." As Goldberg explains, politically correct producers continually put concerns about their racial "virtue" ahead of their concerns about telling the truth. According to Goldberg, his producers were always worried about showing too many black criminals in jail, even when the prison was loaded with black criminals.

The human resources department was directed to devise and enforce a "no personal use of corporate property" policy. In the first test case of this policy, an employee was charged with taking several boxes of paper out of the building. But in his defense, the employee said that the new policy should have been publicized more to give all employees adequate notice. The next case involved a sixty-two-year-old woman who took home a laptop computer for her granddaughter to use in a school project. But the woman was only a year away from retirement, so she was just given a mild warning. Next came a union activist, but there were too many dangers in trying to enforce the policy against that person. Eventually, a black employee was charged. But because all the previous cases had involved white employees who had been given leniency, nothing could be done in this case either. The policy was finally shelved and never used again.

Not surprisingly, the current "racial morality" has not made the world any more racially harmonious or just. Racial segregation and divisiveness is on the rise, just as are accusations of racism. Moreover, the deluge of discrimination claims is actually having an unintended, destructive effect on the broader moral health of society. Although once necessary to dismantle social barricades, the antidiscrimination crusade is now contributing to a moral erosion throughout society. As black community activist Jesse Lee Peterson notes, "Most black folks are not suffering because of racism but because of lack of moral character."[41]

The constant racial attacks against the police have not only eroded the public trust needed for effective law enforcement, but they have actually hurt the people on whose behalf those racial attacks are supposedly being made. Indeed, the attacks have effectively ensured that the poorest and most vulnerable neighborhoods will continue to be ruled by violence. As Heather MacDonald notes, because of racial-data-collection rules, every officer knows that "if he has too many interactions with minority citizens—including responding to crime calls or preventing a mugging—he could face a bias charge."[42] Consequently, some officers will shy away from aggressively fighting crime, leaving inner-city residents at the mercy of violent predators.

Racial justice, in the broader context, is not just about quotas or government programs or even entitlement claims of minority groups. It is about a wider morality—a society's duties to justice, fairness, equality, and civility. Consequently, the broader context of racial justice requires a firmly held code of moral values, not just a collection of rules on discrimination. Yet it is the primacy and ambiguity of such rules that in fact are chipping away at society's moral values.

FIVE

A
Moral
ErosiOn

IDEALLY, DISCRIMINATION claims should have a positive effect on social morality by strengthening the moral character of society. But now that racism has transcended into the realm of the "subtle" and "subconscious," racial discrimination claims have come to exert a corrosive influence on social morality. Now that definitions of racism are all encompassing, the imposition of moral standards that on their face seem racially neutral can nonetheless, at any time, be characterized as racist. Consequently, fearful of the racism label, society hesitates to place any moral or cultural expectations on racial minorities. But that is just the beginning. In a society committed to equality, when racial minorities are relieved of all moral duties, it is a short step to relieving the larger culture of those same duties. This dynamic was demonstrated during the 1960s when white professors, acting under the new spirit of affirmative action, stopped giving low grades to black students. However, to justify or conceal this practice, they also stopped giving low grades to white students.[1]

Because of claims that racism pervades society, nearly every type of moral or cultural standard applied to minorities eventually is shifted to the racial category. But this in turn tends to diminish the independent weight of those standards. Therefore, the issue is whether a suspension of moral and cultural standards for racial minorities will, instead of somehow helping those minorities to succeed, cause a decline in the standards of the larger culture.

A cement-block recreation building stood in the middle of the city park. The north side of the building had no windows, and that was where all the graffiti went. Years ago, the park commissioner tried to crack down on the graffiti. He posted guards, and he prosecuted anyone caught with a can of spray paint. But his crusade didn't last long. Civil rights advocates argued that the crackdown was racially motivated.

After the attacks of September 11, the city erected a monument in the same park. Almost immediately, graffiti started appearing on the monument. But this time, the graffiti was primarily the work of young white males.

The chain of moral erosion begins with the granting of racial exemptions and acquiescing in the claim that the imposition of moral expectations on minorities is a racist act. In a culture in which race defines social morality, traditional notions of moral values become subsumed within prevailing racial sensitivities. Hence, with race superceding traditional morality, accusations of racism can override any attempt to enforce cultural or moral standards. Fearful of incurring charges of racism, society effectively suspends any moral or cultural expectations on minority behavior. But as Christopher Lasch argues, a "respect for cultural diversity" does not automatically forbid us from "imposing the standards of privileged groups on the victims of oppression."[2]

When the Reverend Al Sharpton ran for the Democratic presidential nomination in 2004, he characterized his campaign as representing the disadvantaged and dispossessed. Midway through his campaign, however, a study of candidate expenditures showed that Sharpton on average paid three thousand dollars a night for his personal hotel room.

This was more than three times the average hotel cost incurred by any other candidate, including the president. Yet there was no outrage or even debate concerning this striking disconnect between public proclamation and private deed. But the extravagant hotel bills were just one item. An investigation of the Sharpton campaign by the *New York Times* produced a host of potential violations of election laws.[3] In addition, Sharpton was immersed in a web of financial misdealings, some of which had prompted an audit by the Internal Revenue Service. Several years earlier, in a settlement of various felony charges, he had pled guilty to failing to file personal income taxes. Moreover, a Sharpton-controlled business had an outstanding tax warrant against it for failing to pay New York State unemployment insurance, and another Sharpton corporation had been dissolved for failing to pay taxes throughout most of the 1990s. As the *New York Times* acknowledged, "A financial record like Mr. Sharpton's would probably put an end to most bids for office."[4]

Where race is involved, as if rendering everything else moot, morality considerations seem to evaporate. In September 2004 the Congressional Black Caucus hosted a charity concert to raise money for a college scholarship fund. The featured performer at this concert was R. Kelly, who had recently been indicted on fourteen counts of child pornography. But this apparently did not trouble the preeminent black political organization in the country. A representative of the group, responding to concerns about the moral message that CBC's affiliation with R. Kelly might send, simply stated, "We are confident that Kelly's performance will help us to achieve our goal to educate the next generation of leaders."[5] As it turned out, Kelly's performance attracted two thousand people, including many top legislators. This was similar to the reception given singer Michael Jackson. Shortly after Jackson was indicted on nine counts of lewd acts with a child, he was invited to the nation's capital by Congresswoman Sheila Jackson (D-TX) so that he could be honored by the African Ambassadors' Spouses Association as a "great humanitarian."

The head of the state transportation department was discovered to have taken his mistress to Hawaii on a state-paid trip. But when the news broke, the debate did not focus on the ethics of the act; it centered on whether white bureaucrats in the past had engaged in such behavior and not been punished.

The suspension of cultural or moral judgment on any issue in which race is involved has even occurred within the African American community itself, where a belief in the pervasive racism of society often carries with it a rejection of everything perceived as "white" morality. For instance, when a 2005 article in *Ebony* magazine listed the top ten black couples, only one was a married couple.[6] According to the Reverend Eugene Rivers, an African American minister who counsels disadvantaged youth, the real inner-city black problem is "a moral" one.[7] The "anything-goes sexual morality of the sixties had a disastrous impact on poor blacks," Rivers states, "since it undermined the family life that nurtures the attitudes and habits that lead to success."

As Robert Hampton writes, "Sexual abuse, physical child abuse, and family violence are arguably among the most serious social problems in the black community."[8] Spousal abuse occurs approximately four times as often among blacks as among whites, and the AIDS rate among blacks is three times higher than among the general U.S. population.[9] Noting that moral issues often get swept aside by race, entertainer Bill Cosby describes "the seeming acceptance of having children and not making the father responsible [for them]" as a kind of epidemic.[10] He also criticizes those who rush to defend any black person charged with a crime with the argument that the alleged perpetrator is a victim of racism.

Not only have the constant charges of racism blunted the imposition of moral expectations upon minorities, but the pervasive discrimination mind-set has actually turned traditional moral values into an agent of racism. Consequently, irresponsible and destructive behavior cannot be directly addressed without first traversing the almost uncrossable terrain of racism. Even though one-third of black males will be imprisoned at some time in their lives, even though homicide is the leading cause of death for young black men, the only fault factor that can be discussed is racism.[11] Even though out-of-wedlock births among blacks have grown nearly sevenfold since the Great Depression, any talk of sexual morality or traditional childbearing norms is interpreted as racist, despite the fact that illegitimacy is a major cause of crime, poverty, and disorder in the African American community.[12] Even though civil rights activists argue that it is unfair and unrealistic to expect alienated black youths to be polite to customers, the high unemployment rates among inner-city black youths are portrayed as conclusive evidence of racism.[13]

As Dan Subotnik argues in *Toxic Diversity*, civil rights activists often tend to implicitly celebrate any conduct that violates mainstream middle-class values.[14] When a black student at a Connecticut high school was disciplined for wearing pants that hung so low as to expose his underwear, local civil rights leaders alleged racism, arguing that such pants were the preferred attire of African American males.[15] But this culturally oppositional stance, promoted primarily by white radicals, has seduced poor blacks into a life of poverty and dependency. For instance, even though welfare played a very small role in the life of black America prior to the 1960s, by the late 1970s, blacks constituted 70 percent of all long-term welfare recipients in the country.[16] According to John McWhorter, this was the "first time in black American history that dependency had become a norm," and it occurred "even though economic opportunities were wider than ever before."[17] To justify this culture of dependence, racial activists told young black men that mainstream society wasn't worth their allegiance—a message that in turn drove many of these men to a life of crime.

A career services counselor worked for weeks with a black student. He helped the student draft a résumé. He discussed interview practices and tried to formulate strategies for succeeding in those interviews. But never once did he mention to the student anything about what kinds of clothes to wear or what kind of English grammar to use.

The steady stream of discrimination charges is wearing down society's confidence in its moral capacity. When repeatedly accused of being inherently racist, and hence inherently immoral, people lose confidence in their individual and collective ability to do good. This in turn drives society into a moral emptiness. It suspends moral judgment, making both society and the individual afraid to enforce moral standards. Such a suspension of judgment is particularly evident in the widespread social acceptance of the raw, sexist, violent, and degrading lyrics of certain types of rap music. No moral judgment can be made because of the fear of being tagged with discrimination. (Not surprisingly, the first prominent figure to take a stand against the violent lyrics of rap music is a black leader, the Reverend Al Sharpton.)

A suspension of moral accountability is also occurring at the highest levels of American society. After Mary Frances Berry refused to step down as chair of the U.S. Civil Rights Commission, in defiance of the law, it was revealed that the commission itself had been violating the law for years, ever since Berry had assumed the position of chair, by failing to conduct any independent audits of itself. Because of its status as a civil rights organization combating racism, the commission had never been held accountable for failing to comply with various laws.[18]

Moral values require judgment, which is diametrically opposed to the notion of indiscriminate tolerance—a notion fostered by current racial politics. Also contributing to a repression of moral judgment is the cult of victimhood, which likewise has roots in the discrimination mindset. Under this cult, individuals seek virtue simply by identifying themselves as victims. Whereas the traditional sense of virtue was based on some ideal of perfectibility, the contemporary sense of virtue is based on sin—or more precisely, on being the victim of certain sins, such as discrimination.

The decline in the authority of moral standards was exemplified by the widespread opposition to Vice President Dan Quayle's criticism of the way television glorified single parenthood and dismissed fatherhood. But with 90 percent of welfare families headed by single mothers, there seems an undeniable link between poverty, hardship, and single parenthood—a link that has often been obscured because of society's inability or reluctance to impose moral standards. According to the Heritage Foundation, children born outside of wedlock exhibit 68 percent more antisocial behavior, 78 percent more peer conflict, and 53 percent more dependency. Overall, children of never-married mothers have behavioral problems that score nearly three times higher than children raised in comparable intact families.[19] Indeed, the theory that single-parent families are desirable alternative lifestyles was not invented by single mothers but by intellectuals who believed they were removing a stigma from an oppressed class.[20] Moreover, the notion that single parenthood should be exalted in the name of diversity ignores the fact that, according to James Wilson in *Home-Alone America,* more than half of all children are now being raised in single-parent homes.

THE MORAL and cultural dilemma now posed by America's racial attitudes was predicted by Patrick Moynihan in 1965.[21] Citing the increasing erosion of the black family, Moynihan revealed what happens when a society begins suspending the moral and cultural standards by which it judges itself. Afraid of appearing racist, society "defines deviancy down"—a process by which pathological behavior such as high crime rates and illegitimacy become socially acceptable. As Moynihan warned, "A community that allows a large number of young men to grow up in broken families, dominated by women, never acquiring any stable relationship to male authority . . . asks for and gets chaos." Indeed, that is what has happened, but by criticizing certain aspects of black culture, Moynihan was branded a racist.[22]

The cultural problems outlined by Moynihan four decades ago are no longer just African American problems; they have spilled over into the rest of the culture and are now national problems. Since 1965, crime rates in society at large have risen faster than crime rates in the black community. This is also true for illegitimacy and teen pregnancy. The white illegitimacy rate today is approximately the same as the African American rate in 1965; the rate for Hispanics now exceeds that of blacks.[23] Roughly a third of all American births are to single women.[24] In fact, white women under the age of twenty-five are more likely to have a child out of wedlock than in.[25] Meanwhile, cultural conditions in the black community have continued to deteriorate. Whereas in 1960 78 percent of all black families were headed by married couples, that figure has been cut in half. Indeed, the dismantling of moral codes has been most destructive to minorities. The black illegitimacy rate, for instance, shot up to its present high level only after the 1960s and the advent of moral relativism.[26]

As Charles Krauthammer argues, the cultural tendency to "define deviancy down" has actually caused a moral inversion, in which traditional institutions such as heterosexual courtship and the family are treated as deviant settings for sexual abuse and domestic violence.[27] This moral inversion, or social demoralization, as historian Gertrude Himmelfarb calls it, is a direct result of the denial of moral and civilizational norms.[28] Because once a society suspends moral or cultural standards for racial minorities, it eventually has to make those same suspensions for the wider society; for if moral values lose their legitimacy for one group, they lose their legitimacy for all. But under the current "every judgment can be a racist one" mentality, how are society's leaders supposed to react when people further down the social ladder—particularly if they are racial minorities—are drifting into a culture that is degrading?

A society cannot have two different codes of behavior—one for racial minorities and one for the majority culture. Social norms are like water; they quickly level out to the lowest common level. This is one reason why white youths, attracted to the ability of their black counterparts to rebel against social rules, have increasingly adopted the antisocial mentality of the black urban underclass. Whites are attracted to rap music "because of its rebellious and anti-establishment themes."[29] This phenomenon is illustrated in Adam Mansbach's novel *Angry Black White Boy* in which the author satirizes wealthy white youths who seek their authenticity through black hip-hop. In the novel, the main character, a preadolescent white boy, is enraged at the acquittal of the white police officers charged with assaulting Rodney King. Though wanting to "make his contribution to the struggle by providing whiteness for the stomping," the boy cannot find any black people in his neighborhood who could stomp on him. So he then tries to start his own riot.

Joan was the teacher with the least seniority, so it was her job to monitor the north playground during morning recess. She hated it, sometimes to the point of wanting to quit her job. The kids played the music so loud, and it was impossible not to hear the lyrics. She tried to pretend she was absorbed in her magazine, but she sensed that the kids knew what she was doing.

A few weeks earlier, she had confiscated a child's music player—she was outraged, even embarrassed, by the raw lyrics of the rapper. Afterward, the older teachers laughed at her; they said only a naive newcomer would make that mistake. There were complaints, accusations, a few meetings, and even a hearing. She had no right to impose her tastes, a parent said. She had no right to single out children by their race, a community activist charged. When it was all over, Joan was told that she was simply to keep the peace on the playground. Don't let anyone get hurt, stop the fights before they begin, be on the lookout for sexual groping, the principal said.

Joan could tell that the children were flaunting their triumph over her. It used to be that only one or two children listened to that kind of music. Now, more than half of them did.

Author Tom Wolfe describes an America witnessing a "gradual disappearance of conventional morality."[30] And because of this moral erosion, it is often difficult to see the larger moral aspects of any public issue. This difficulty is apparent with the issue of stem cell research, in which the larger moral issue of whether such research involves tampering with human life has virtually been ignored. A similar blindness has occurred with the war on terror, which is often perceived only as a matter of safety and not as a moral confrontation between the forces of democracy and those of tyranny. Indeed, contemporary vocabulary reflects an incapacity of moral vision. In place of words like *right* or *wrong* are less precise and judgmental words, such as *appropriate* and *inappropriate*—words that once applied to wearing brown shoes in public after 6 p.m.

With no sound belief in society's moral capacity, there cannot be any call to moral action. If fears of racism charges cause America to doubt its moral authority on the matter of illegal immigration, for instance, it will be unable to take any action on that issue. And even though political activists call health care a moral issue, there is no moral direction on how to proceed. With its moral confidence eroded by all the accusations of discrimination involving medical treatment delivered to racial minorities, society is helpless to approach health care as a moral issue.

There is a similar lack of moral energy in the fight against school violence. One and a half million incidents of violence at public schools occurred during the 1999–2000 school year alone,[31] and the cause of this violence was often attributed to racism. During the 1950s, however, there were single-parent households and poverty and societal discrimination, and yet today's levels of violence would have been unimaginable then. But the violence is tolerated now because to act against it is to risk charges of discrimination. So what remains are unsafe schools that breed brutality and indifference rather than intellectual development and emotional maturity.

IT IS not just moral values that get suffocated by racism allegations; even issues involving national security can be overridden by fears of discrimination charges. Such charges have stymied the nation's attempt to deal with illegal immigration as a national security threat. As the 9/11 Commission found, "The challenge for national security in an age of terrorism is to prevent the very few people who may pose overwhelming risks from entering or remaining in the United States undetected." Yet all attempts to curtail illegal immigration into America have been met with accusations of racial discrimination. Civil rights activists portray as racist anyone who supports secure borders, enforced immigration laws, and penalties imposed on people who break those laws. Falling under the umbrella of acts accused of being racist are a proposal to add two thousand new Border Patrol agents, an expansion of illegal alien detention facility space, an increase in the number of foreign airports with counterterrorist passenger screening programs, a toughening of the penalties for using false identification documents, a reduction in the bureaucratic delays allowing illegal aliens who obtained fraudulent visas to remain in the country even after their visas have been revoked, and a requirement that asylum seekers tied to terrorist organizations provide credible proof of their "persecution."[32]

Father Michael Branson was the pastor of St. Mary's Catholic parish. It was a parish with an unusual membership: approximately half were white and half were recent immigrants from Asia and Latin America. Father Branson had taken the lead in a crusade to convince state government to issue education vouchers that could be used by low-income citizens to pay their children's tuition at the school of their choice. His traditional-minded immigrant parishioners had pushed him to lead that crusade; they saw the public schools as places where their children would be exposed to morally offensive ideas and the constant presence of violence and drugs. All they wanted was for their children to get a good education, they told Father Branson.

The crusade was gaining ground. Its support was spreading, and a legislative committee had agreed to hold hearings. But then something happened. It was as if a bucket of water had suddenly been thrown on a flame. The finance director of the diocese in which St. Mary's was situated announced that he had received a complaint from a black parishioner at St.

Mary's, alleging that the parish had discriminated against her in the disbursal of charity funds. The finance director reiterated that the diocese would not tolerate racism in any fashion and that Father Branson would be suspended from his duties while an investigation proceeded.

A week later, nearly 60 percent of St. Mary's white parishioners demanded that Father Branson be permanently withdrawn as pastor. But only a small number of immigrant parishioners signed the petition, even though they were disappointed that the hearing on the voucher bill had been canceled.

Discrimination charges against one individual can often taint entire social institutions. But when enough institutions are tainted, the whole culture becomes morally suspect as well as the values they promote. And when all social institutions lose their public respect, they lose their authority. And when social institutions lack authority, the vital machinery of society breaks down. As William Galston argues, "Every society is weakened by the diminution of its members' belief in its legitimacy."[33]

To the extent that racial discrimination charges have become so pervasive as to be unsupported by reality, they exert a corrosive effect on social institutions. Indeed, the continued barrage of discrimination charges being levied against every type of social institution has coincided with a decline in public regard for those institutions. As Heather MacDonald notes, "Surely the cops would get more support from the community if their moral authority were not constantly under siege."[34]

If, as the cultural Left so often accuses, every institution in America is completely infected with the racism virus, then perhaps there is no remedial action possible. Perhaps all that can be done is to scrap everything and start over. Perhaps the only way to save society is to destroy it. On the other hand, if society and its institutions are not so irrevocably imbued with racism, then they are being unfairly and perhaps irreparably damaged by the taint of racism—a stain that in turn is causing a moral downgrading to all of society. (Indeed, attacking all social institutions so as to attack incidents of racism is like destroying the house in order to get rid of the rat in the basement.) Even though racial discrimination charges seem on the surface to be a harmless-at-worst attempt to achieve social justice, they can (if false) have a much more destructive effect.

Because of its moral role, religion is a social institution much affected by the moral implications of racism charges. Ironically, the more a religion espouses traditional values, the more racially suspect it has become. The religiously devout, especially evangelical Christians, are often categorically accused of harboring racist attitudes. Indeed, the only praise given to religious organizations seems to be when they engage in the fight against racism. Compare, for instance, the universal acclaim given to Martin Luther King Jr.'s "God is marching on" speech—in which he called for electing legislators who "walk humbly with their God"—with the deafening criticism given to religious leaders who speak out on such issues as abortion, gay marriage, and individual virtue.

The role of race in determining the public image of religion can also be seen in the ways African American churches are treated differently from predominately white churches. When politicians appear at black churches to solicit political support, or when black leaders use their churches to hold political fund-raisers, the efforts are praised as valuable civic activism. But when similar functions occur at white churches, they are condemned as violating the separation of church and state. This racial double standard between religions can be further seen in the actions of a Colorado school district that removed books on Christianity from a classroom while allowing books on Native American religion to remain.

Religious institutions seem to attract public acclaim not when they perform any of their traditional spiritual or charity functions but only when they espouse the racially correct position. Just as President Clinton embraced the black community during his impeachment crisis, religious organizations preach the racism message whenever they wish to rehabilitate their public image or seek redemption for prior sins. Even for religion, the one way to attain social redemption for whatever other wrongs may have once been committed is to confess the one universal sin—racism. In the wake of all the publicity regarding the sexual abuse scandals in the Catholic Church, for instance, Archbishop Harry Flynn released a high-profile pastoral letter stating that organized religion has often fostered attitudes of racial superiority.[35] Black leaders praised Flynn's actions, saying that "the Catholic Church has been silent too long" (even though more than twenty years earlier the Catholic bishops of the United States had issued a similar pastoral letter on racism, and even though the first diocesan pastoral letter condemning racism was published in 1956 by the archbishop of New Orleans, who later excommunicated several prominent segregationists for refusing to follow the church's teaching that racism was wrong).

Bishop Flynn's evidence of racism amounted in large part to anecdotal stories, including one involving his hesitancy as a child to invite an African American girl to his birthday party. But are these portrayals of past racism truly indicative of what Flynn describes as present-day institutional racism in the Catholic Church?[36] Flynn goes on to repeat the "racism by statistics" argument: parishes tend to be somewhat culturally and racially homogenous, because parishes reflect the demographics of their surrounding neighborhoods, because blacks do not make up a significant portion of Catholic parish membership, therefore the Catholic Church is a perpetrator of racism. In an indictment of all religion, Flynn writes, "Ten o'clock on Sunday morning is one of the most segregated hours in American society."[37] Based on his anecdotal evidence, he condemns "the racism that we find embedded in the social, economic, political, and cultural institutions of society."[38] But in this attempt to attain some social redemption for the recent sins of the Catholic Church, Flynn universally tainted and discredited all religious institutions.

David belonged to the ACLU. He was a lawyer. In his last case, he had prevented a Christian evangelical group from conducting a prayer session in a public park adjacent to city hall.

David was also a member of the NAACP. During the Reverend Lutwan Harris's "Spiritual Uplift Revival," David was given a reserved seat under the huge tent that had been erected in the park where the revival was held.

David was white.

There are no longer the seven deadly sins—there is just one sin, discrimination, with all other values or virtues secondary. But this has left society so devoid of public morality that, for example, there is no audience backlash against celebrities who commit morally repulsive acts. As long as they preach against discrimination, celebrities need not worry about their moral behavior or any public reaction to it. Since race confers absolute moral virtue, the "correct" attitudes on race essentially enable one to do anything he or she wants regarding any other area of moral behavior. But this "one sin only" focus does not and cannot fulfill the broader function of teaching society how to be more moral or virtuous. There is even reason to doubt that the current "racial correctness" can achieve its most elemental objectives. A survey by Stanley Rothman and Seymour Martin Lipset shows that the more racial diversity is emphasized on a college campus, the less enthusiastic students are about the quality of education at that campus. Furthermore, Rothman and Lipset found that such diversity-focused schools actually experienced more reports of discrimination, not less.[39]

As the authors of *The Federalist Papers* explained more than two hundred years ago, a democracy requires a higher degree of virtue in its citizens than does any other form of government.[40] According to William Galston, a democracy "cannot be wholly indifferent to the character of its citizens," since its viability "depends on its ability to engender a virtuous citizenry."[41] As Harvey Mansfield observes, a free society cannot survive if its people are so free that nothing is expected of them. Democracies also depend on a certain level of civility and trust among its citizens; once destroyed, this trust and civility cannot be imposed by legal dictates. Discrimination charges, rightly so, must seek justice. But this pursuit is not free. If conducted carelessly, it can undermine such necessary democratic traits as trust and civility.

Under the antidiscrimination mind-set, the sole focus is on freeing people from outside constraints rather than on strengthening civic virtue or the social institutions of moral education. With antidiscrimination as the primary component of public morality, the litany of rights tends to eclipse any dialogue of duties or public discussion about virtue.[42] Consequently, all self-restraint values have fallen victim to self-liberation concerns. As Robert Wuthnow observes, "The language of sacrifice has dropped out of our vocabulary" because of all the emphasis on self.[43]

The failure of the current maze of racial rules to breed a larger moral framework can be seen in the anger and hypocrisy that have developed regarding race. Instead of reflecting a stronger commitment to racial peace and harmony, civil rights activists are simply resorting to old racial divisions and bigotries. At a time when racial stereotypes and racial attacks were supposed to be taboo, for instance, Democrats responded to George W. Bush's running mate selection by deriding Dick Cheney as a balding, overweight "old white guy." Even *Time* magazine ridiculed Cheney as an old "white guy with a paunch." Jesse Jackson implied that Cheney was a racist solely on the grounds that Cheney was white, male, and conservative. But the moral emptiness and double standards of contemporary cultural attitudes on racial discrimination will certainly not bring about the kind of racial justice and morality for which Martin Luther King Jr. once hoped.

SIX

The Political
PerpetuatIon
of Racism

RACISM STARTED out as an issue of human rights, and the fight against racism became a crusade for social justice. But now racism has grown into a political lifeline for America's oldest political party.

The ideological identity of the Democratic Party hinges largely on race. And combating racial discrimination sits atop the party's proclaimed agenda. The civil rights crusade, along with the sexual revolution and the antiwar movement, gave birth to the modern Democratic Party. Even now, when party leaders wish to energize their base and sanctify their cause, they deliver the sermon of racial justice and revive the image of America's civil rights struggles. Senator John Edwards (D-NC) did this in his speech at the 2004 Democratic National Convention, when he spoke of 1950s-style segregation as if it were still a reality in contemporary America.

In accepting his party's nomination for president, John Kerry (D-MA) said that it was "time to reject the kind of politics calculated to divide race from race." But that is just what the Democrats have been doing for years—creating and then exploiting racial divisions for their own political advantage, implying that nothing in America has changed since the days of the Ku Klux Klan and the night riders. Perhaps that is why the Democratic Party never admits that any progress has been made in America's race relations: because to do so would jeopardize one of the sustaining pillars of the party.

Not only is the fight against racism an ideologically defining feature of the Democratic Party, it is perhaps the only trump-card issue "owned" by Democrats—an issue that, when played, trumps any other political argument or opposition. It is also an issue that attracts a vital constituency. To hold this constituency, however, the party must continually keep alive the threatening specter of racism. This brandishing of generalized and ambiguous racism charges is one of the Democrats' most successful political strategies—one they have used to create a "racism coalition" made up of racial minorities and recent immigrant groups.

Such a coalition depends almost exclusively on the issue of racism, since on many other social issues the Democratic Party is out of step with immigrants and African Americans. On abortion, school prayer, faith-based government programs, and school vouchers, blacks have long stood to the right of the Democratic Party.[1] For instance, 66 percent of blacks favor school vouchers.[2] And with respect to gay rights, blacks are far more conservative than whites. According to a December 2003 poll, 75 percent of blacks oppose same-sex marriage, compared with 59 percent of whites.[3] Indeed, a deep theological and social conservatism characterizes most black protestant churches, with African Americans more likely than other Americans to treat the Bible as literal truth.[4]

Even on economic matters, Democratic policies have not coincided with the long-term interests of many poor African Americans. From 1971 to 1995, the poverty rate for children of single mothers fell only slightly, from 53.1 percent to 50.3 percent. But in just the five years after passage of the 1996 welfare reform act, the figure dropped to a record low of 39.8 percent. In 2005, there were almost three million fewer children living in poverty than there were in 1995. Despite this success, however, many Democrats still refused to support the welfare reform act.

Race has become a potent political weapon. It is a simple weapon, an all-purpose weapon, a weapon that does not require any supporting ammunition. During the 2004 campaign, John Kerry branded Attorney General John Ashcroft as a racist, but if Democrats really believed the attorney general was racist, they would surely have brought formal charges. Kerry also accused President Bush of being a racial divider by opposing mandatory affirmative action rules, despite the fact that twelve years earlier Kerry had criticized affirmative action on the grounds that it had created a "culture of dependency" and had divisively "kept America thinking in racial terms." In a speech to the Congressional Black Caucus in 2004, Kerry said that President Bush was taking America back to a segregationist age. He said there was a "Do not enter" sign on the White House door to keep out blacks, despite the president's record number of minority appointments to high governmental positions. Even Senator Zell Miller (D-GA) was accused of being a racist after his speech at the Republican National Convention endorsing George Bush, despite the fact that Miller, as governor of Georgia, had appointed more African Americans to the state judiciary than had Jimmy Carter.[5]

The human suffering caused by Hurricane Katrina in 2005 provided yet another political opportunity for racism charges. Jesse Jackson and a host of civil rights activists attributed the inadequacies of the federal relief effort to racism. Randall Robinson proclaimed that "black hurricane victims" were feeding on human corpses after just three or four days without food.[6] Even though New Orleans's population was two-thirds black, with a poverty rate of 25 percent, the fact that so many of the victims of the hurricane were poor blacks was blamed on racism within a Republican administration in Washington. Indeed, the very occurrence of the trauma seemed to be chalked up to governmental racism toward a predominantly black city. But this ignores previous natural disasters, such as Hurricane Andrew, where a quarter of a million residents, mostly white, were left homeless—and where people went without food and power for five days, just as they did in New Orleans. In the aftermath of Andrew, the Federal Emergency Management Agency (FEMA) was likewise blamed for incompetence in the slowness of its relief effort, but what was missing there, because most of the victims were white, was the racial allegation.

Besides furnishing the cause of the human suffering wrought by Katrina, racism also provided cover for all the savagery and violence that occurred in the hurricane's aftermath. The looting of stores, the shooting at rescue helicopters, and the gang attacks on hospitals were all attributed to the effects of racism. Roaming gangs reportedly used racial taunts during their looting.[7] Such taunts apparently expressed the belief that the stealing and looting were not criminal deeds but acts of restitution for all the racial wrongs done to these gang members. And yet what a behavioral contrast the reaction in New Orleans was to that of the tsunami that caused such incalculable damage throughout coastal Southeast Asia.

Democrats often paint Republicans as cross-burners who want to deny African American children any chance at an education, as hate-mongers who drag black men to their death behind pickup trucks, and as fascist zealots who want to incarcerate as many blacks as possible. As one liberal professor told his class at the University of Colorado, the R in Republican stands for "racist."[8] During the 2000 presidential campaign, the NAACP sponsored an attack ad that linked the 1998 dragging death of James Byrd, a black Texan, to George Bush's failure as governor to strengthen a Texas hate-crime law. In 2004, filmmaker Michael Moore, who shared a box at the Democratic Convention with former president Jimmy Carter, described Republicans as being "up at six in the morning trying to figure out which minority group they're going to screw today."[9] Indeed, to listen to the racial accusations made by Democrats in the twenty-first century is to hear the name Hitler and the word *Nazi* spoken almost as frequently as they were in the 1930s. And yet when it comes to black conservatives, Democrats readily stir up the hate.

NAACP president Kweisi Mfume described George Bush's black supporters as "ventriloquists' dummies," suggesting that they were mindless mouthpieces for a racially divisive president.[10] Previously, former

NAACP head Benjamin Hooks had called African American conservatives "some of the biggest liars the world ever saw."[11] During his campaign for lieutenant governor of Maryland, black Republican Michael Steele was the target of Oreo cookies thrown onto the stage by supporters of his opponent—a gesture intended to slur Steele as a betrayer of his race, a man "black on the outside, white on the inside."[12] The Black Congressional Caucus once tried to punish Gary Franks, a black Republican member of Congress, for holding "racially traitorous views."[13] More recently, President Bush's nominations of Miguel Estrada (a Hispanic) and Janice Rogers Brown (an African American) were depicted as attacks on minority rights since those nominees were described as having judicial philosophies at odds with the liberal civil rights agenda. Senator Edward Kennedy (D-MA) called President Bush's minority judicial nominees "Neanderthals."[14] And Senator Harry Reid (D-NV), the Democratic leader in the Senate, described Justice Clarence Thomas as "an embarrassment" to the Supreme Court, contrasting Thomas's incompetence with Justice Scalia's "brilliance of mind."[15]

A particularly vile liberal attack on a black conservative was aimed at the first black female secretary of state, Condoleeza Rice.[16] Liberal satirists depicted Rice as an "ebonics-speaking, big-lipped, black mammy who just loves her massa," and a liberal talk-show host called Rice an "Aunt Jemima."[17] These uses of racial stereotypes were denounced by a coalition of black clergy.[18] According to the Reverend Jesse Lee Peterson, the leader of a black family outreach program, Democrats "pretend that racism is holding back black Americans, but [Democrats] are doing all they can to hold back [African Americans like Condoleeza Rice, simply] because her views or principles don't coincide with theirs."[19]

Democrats exploit the white fear of being called racist, even though Democrats are the first to lob those allegations. This is illustrated with the illegal immigration issue. In trying to garner the immigrant vote, Democrats accuse anyone who opposes illegal immigration as racist. They have been so successful at equating conservatives with racists that blatant double standards have evolved. For instance, when Democratic senator Christopher Dodd (D-CT) praised Senator Robert Byrd (D-WV) as a man who "would have been a great leader at any moment" in history, he received almost no criticism, even though Byrd had once been a member of the Ku Klux Klan and had tried to derail the 1964 Civil Rights Act.[20] Yet two years earlier, when Senator Trent Lott (R-MS) gave a speech praising Strom Thurmond (R-SC) at a party celebrating Thurmond's one hundredth birthday, Lott was forced to resign his position as Senate majority leader because Thurmond had run for president on a segregationist platform in 1948. Nor was Governor Howard Dean criticized by fellow Democrats for the racial stereotype he used in a speech to black Democrats, when he said "the Republican National Committee could only get this many people of color in a single room if they had the hotel staff in here."[21]

A racial double standard has also been applied to the political activities of religious groups. During the 2004 presidential campaign, George Bush was roundly criticized for his outreach to evangelical Christians.[22] Democrats called the effort "an exploitation of religious faith for political gain." And yet, in an effort to bring out the black vote, the Kerry campaign instituted a "souls to polls" program aimed at recruiting voters from black churches as well as another program in which local ministers would lead carpools of parishioners to cast early votes after Sunday services.[23] Obviously, black churches are not held to the same degree of "church-state separation" that white churches are held. This was evident during Jesse Jackson's presidential campaign, when he held fund-raisers in the black churches of Chicago without any objections from the ACLU or other civil libertarian groups.[24]

There is nothing unifying about the Democrats' racial politics. Instead of ever highlighting the opportunities blacks now have or the progress they've made, Democrats use a divide-and-conquer strategy to make blacks feel disconnected from the success and prosperity of America, even though black homeownership is at an all-time high, as is black membership in the middle class. But this message of disconnect only tells minorities that they are not part of the wider culture of America, that they have no stake in or allegiance to it. As the Reverend Jesse Lee Peterson observes in *Scam: How the Black Leadership Exploits Black America,* the civil rights establishment has made a lucrative career out of keeping racial strife alive in America. And in this respect, scholar and author Shelby Steele does not "expect anything to change until the current civil rights leadership just dies off."[25] According to Steele, this leadership is "concerned with nothing except keeping their people in the Democratic Party. . . . It's gotten to the point where we've now made affiliation with the Democratic Party an aspect of the black American identity."

The use of race as a political strategy was particularly apparent in the Democratic allegations regarding disenfranchisement of minority voters during the 2004 presidential campaign. By claiming that Republicans were out to deliberately deny blacks the right to vote, Democrats resurrected the most heinous wrongs of America's past. A fund-raising letter sent by Senator Jon Corzine (D-NJ) claimed that "the GOP used voter intimidation and outright fraud to hand Florida to George W. Bush in 2000, and if we don't stop them, they'll do it again." Democratic activists described the refusal of a county election officer to let black voters redo incomplete voter registrations as reminiscent of a blocked schoolhouse door at the height of desegregation, even though the real blame for the incomplete registrations lay with the voter-registration groups that had turned in the "sloppy" forms.[26]

Ever since losing the 2000 presidential election, Democrats have alleged that African American voters have been systematically disenfranchised by a discriminatory voting system. This accusation, however, directly contradicts the evidence. In June 2001, the U.S. Commission on Civil Rights issued a report that found no evidence of voter intimidation and no evidence of intentional or systematic disenfranchisement of black voters. The Justice Department's Civil Rights Division conducted a separate investigation that produced a similar conclusion. In a May 2002 letter to Senator Pat Leahy (D-VT), who at the time headed the

Judiciary Committee, Assistant Attorney General Ralph Boyd wrote that "no credible evidence" had been found that Floridians were intentionally denied their right to vote during the November 2000 election. Furthermore, as John Fund points out in *Stealing Elections: How Voter Fraud Threatens Our Democracy*, every recount conducted after the 2000 election showed that George W. Bush won the Florida vote.

Despite these investigations and their conclusions, John Kerry in 2004 warned that Republicans were once again trying to suppress the black vote after having "stolen" one million black votes in 2000. Representative Jesse Jackson Jr. (D-IL) called Republicans "voter terrorists."[27] Democratic National Committee chair Terry McAuliffe accused Republicans of engaging in "systematic efforts" to disenfranchise minority voters. The Democratic group Americans Coming Together handed out flyers depicting an African American on the receiving end of a fire-hose blast. On one side, the flyer read: "This is what they used to do to keep us from voting." On the reverse side, along with a list of alleged incidents of voter intimidation, appeared the warning: "This is how Republicans keep African Americans from voting now." Even former president Jimmy Carter accused Republicans of throwing out "several thousand ballots of African Americans" in 2000. But since ballots are secret and in no way indicate the race of the voter, it is difficult to know how Carter could make such a claim. Moreover, in twenty-four of the twenty-five Florida counties with the highest ballot spoilage rate, the officials in charge of the election process were Democrats.[28]

Charges of racial discrimination were even asserted against Republican election officials who are African American. Ohio Secretary of State Kenneth Blackwell was accused of voter intimidation after he issued a series of orders concerning the type of paper required for mail-in voter registration cards and the procedures election officials should use with voters who appear at the wrong polling place. Democrats claimed that these orders could lead to voter "confusion" and hence "disenfranchisement."[29] Jesse Jackson likened Blackwell to the infamous racist Bull Connor, because of Blackwell's defense of rules prohibiting election workers from giving ballots to voters who were not at their correct polling place.

Just about any measures aimed at providing security at polling places or preventing voter fraud were depicted as efforts to intimidate voters. The claim was made that the mere sight of police officers at the polls was enough to scare off African American voters. Similarly, requiring identification or proof of residency was said to discriminate against minorities who would somehow be traumatized by such requests, even though minorities apparently have no trouble in producing a photo ID when buying an airline ticket or renting a video, and even though no real-life examples of specific individuals who have been so disenfranchised have ever been produced. A Rasmussen Research poll conducted in June 2004 found that 82 percent of Americans believe voters should show a photo ID, but Democratic activist groups contend that such a requirement harasses minority voters. According to Jesse Durfee, chairman of the San Diego Democratic Party, photo ID requirements are "a racist mechanism."

Despite the months of allegations concerning voter discrimination, the 2004 elections occurred without any evidence of systemic minority disenfranchisement.[30] Furthermore, the isolated precincts in which pre-election voter intimidation was alleged to have taken place were primarily those in which Democrats were in charge. Yet even though voter disenfranchisement was practically nonexistent, evidence of voter fraud was overwhelming. In *Stealing Elections: How Voter Fraud Threatens Our Democracy*, John Fund reveals that voter rolls in many cities now contain names of more registered voters than there are residents.[31] In New Mexico, more than a month before the election, officials in one county stated that they had received more than three thousand suspicious registration forms from liberal activist groups.

Not only did all their vocal concern about voter disenfranchisement not prevent Democrats from at least tacitly encouraging voter registration fraud, it also failed to inspire Democrats to do anything about the rash of drive-by shootings, theft, vandalism, and physical attacks committed by anti-Bush partisans. In the weeks preceding the election, there were widespread incidents of violence at Republican campaign offices around the country: burglaries in Seattle and Spokane; break-ins at Cincinnati and Flagstaff; shots fired into offices in Florida, Tennessee, and West Virginia; vandalism of offices in Alaska, Illinois, Montana, and Ohio; a swastika burned into the lawn of a Bush supporter in Madison, Wisconsin; a Republican chairperson assaulted in his office in Gainesville, Florida. In Orlando, a group of Democrats stormed the Bush headquarters and injured several Republican campaign workers. On election day at a Wisconsin GOP headquarters, the tires of thirty "get out the vote" cars were slashed. And at a North Carolina Republican office, a mob of vandals broke windows and left vulgar messages.

The way Democrats used race during the 2004 elections turned out to be a divisive and destructive endeavor. The allegations went not just to the workings of the voting system but to the very integrity of American democracy. By laying the groundwork for refusing to accept any close election that went against them, Democrats were able to cast widespread skepticism about the viability and legitimacy of the democratic process. And in doing so, they undermined the foundation of democratic rule—that the losers accept the verdict of the majority.

A 2004 mobilization plan issued by the Democratic National Committee a month before the election instructed party operatives to "launch preemptive strikes" charging voter intimidation even if there was no evidence that any intimidation was taking place. Consequently, in the weeks leading up to the election, nearly every battleground state was hit with a barrage of lawsuits claiming that the enforcement of voting rules amounted to racial discrimination. Three weeks prior to the election, Florida was "already teeming with lawsuits charging the state and its county elections supervisors with voter disenfranchisement."[32] Similar lawsuits in Michigan and Ohio sought to overturn longstanding rules regarding provisional ballots, claiming that such rules were intended to suppress the minority vote.[33]

Democrats even asked international observers to monitor the U.S. elections for evidence of voter intimidation in the same way that elections in places like Afghanistan and Russia and Venezuela are monitored.[34] Thus, the world's oldest democracy was reduced to the same level as some of the world's most fragile and fledgling democracies. Just as they use race to discredit society and its values, Democrats used it to discredit the electoral system—the institution at the heart of democratic rule.

For months preceding the 2004 election, the repeated attacks on America's electoral institution had such a corrosive effect on public confidence that the nation's news outlets were filled with stories of people fearing that their votes would not be counted. Eighty percent of African Americans believed they would be disenfranchised. But perhaps the most real and damaging effect of the rash of discrimination and disenfranchisement charges lies in how those charges led to a diminished enforcement of voting rules, which in turn contributed to widespread voter registration fraud.

The panicked rush to prevent any discriminatory disenfranchisement of voters effectively resulted in the indiscriminate enfranchisement of untold numbers of illegal aliens, including suspected al Qaeda operatives and terrorist sympathizers. In October 2004, for instance, the *Columbus Dispatch* reported that illegal alien Nuradin Abdi, the suspected shopping mall bomb plotter from Somalia, had been registered to vote in Ohio by a left-wing activist group named ACORN. Also on the Ohio voting rolls was convicted al Qaeda agent Iyman Faris.[35]

This enfranchisement of otherwise illegal voters was a result of all the attacks on voting rules and registration requirements. In Florida, the ACLU filed a lawsuit challenging the constitutionality of a state law that required the posting of a list of "voter rights and responsibilities" in every voting station. Among the listed responsibilities that the ACLU considered racially discriminatory was the requirement to bring proper identification to the polling place.[36] In Iowa, the attorney general ruled that individuals showing up at the wrong voting place would still be permitted to cast a ballot, even if poll workers were unable to verify that the person was eligible to vote. And across the country, the Democratic Party and a host of left-wing activist groups assigned armies of lawyers to stand guard at polling places, ready to make harassment and intimidation accusations against election officials who insisted on voter compliance with certain election laws.

But lost amid all the charges of voter discrimination was the very sanctity of the voting process. Lost were the issues of why something as important as voting cannot carry even the requirement of producing identification of any kind, and why the election process cannot be protected from people who have no right to vote or who have failed to comply with the minimal requirements of voting. Lost was the corrosive effect that voter fraud can have on the perceived legitimacy of democratic elections. Indeed, if illegally cast votes ended up determining the outcome of an election, those illegal ballots would have effectively disenfranchised legally cast votes.

The accusations made by Democrats about racial discrimination in the 2004 election bore an eerie similarity to Democratic accusations eight years earlier concerning racially motivated arson at black churches.

After a number of fires at black churches in 1996, President Clinton proclaimed that a conspiracy of racial hate was to blame and compared the fires with ethnic violence in Bosnia and Rwanda. Even though he had no evidence of any conspiracy, Clinton said it was "clear that racial hostility" was the cause of the fires. In the following days, his administration continued to claim that the country was in the grip of "an epidemic of terror . . . inspired by a resurgence of racial hatred and with clear conspiratorial overtones."[37] Democrats blamed Republicans, suggesting that the fires were the result of a hardening racism "inspired by conservative attempts to end affirmative action, to push hard-line policies on crime, and to radically reform the welfare system." Jesse Jackson claimed that conservatives had "created a climate that was directly responsible for the church burnings."[38] (This was the same Jackson who would later pronounce the tragic hanging death of a seventeen-year-old Mississippi black male to be a racial "lynching." Jackson not only made this pronouncement without a shred of evidence, but he did so after an autopsy had already concluded that the death was suicide.)

Subsequent investigations of the church fires, however, did not support these accusations of racial hate. In an exhaustive study, USA Today found nothing to support the existence of a national conspiracy or of any active involvement of hate groups, or even of a general increase in racial animosity among whites toward blacks.[39] Employing one of its largest task forces in history, the Justice Department also found no trace of a racial conspiracy. Yet even after the task force had issued its report, Vice President Al Gore declared that "1996 was a terrifying year, [when] we witnessed a blaze of violence that seared the nation's conscience."[40]

Two years later, however, the same unwarranted fears were still being stoked. During the congressional elections of 1998, and in the midst of the Clinton impeachment, Missouri Democrats ran an ad on black radio that proclaimed, "When you don't vote, you let another church explode." In addition, Clinton's Justice Department, without a shred of evidence, charged that Republicans were planning to "intimidate" black voters at the polls. But once the election took place, no instances of such intimidation were reported.

During his presidency, Bill Clinton spoke often about ending racial division, but he never said a word when his own Justice Department concluded that the church fires had not been acts of racial hate. Nor did any apologies come from Jesse Jackson or any other Democrat who had accused Republicans of creating a climate of racial hatred that had directly led to the fires.

RACISM HAS been used not only as a political tool to attract constituent groups and discredit the opposition but as a key component in a much wider struggle by the cultural Left to root out the "repressive" influence of traditional moral and cultural values. Beginning in the 1960s, with the civil rights and antiwar movements, many on the Left came to see America as a place of oppression, intolerance, and imperial tyranny.[41] They adopted a victim mentality that focused on all the evils America perpetrates. With the civil rights crusade, liberals viewed America as inherently racist, not as a nation whose constitutional liberties could heal the injustices of the past. With Vietnam, they saw America as a dangerous imperialist, not as the defender of South Vietnam. In Watergate, they saw America as prone to corruption as Soviet-style dictatorships, not as a constitutional democracy capable of holding even its president accountable to the law. And through the feminist movement, they saw America as a place hostile to anyone but a privileged few, not as a society willing to expand its opportunities to all citizens. To the cultural Left, there was so much wrong with the character and identity of America that a complete transformation was needed. The old had to be completely thrown out; moral values that had long shaped American society had to be overthrown; religious organizations that perpetuated these moral values had to be marginalized; historical notions of individual virtue had to be discredited. Having provided a false moral cover to centuries of American repression, all these values and institutions had to be broken down.

This cultural revolution, however, could only be accomplished with a powerful weapon—a weapon for which there was no defense and which struck at the heart of American sensitivities. Such a weapon was found in racism. Even though mainstream society might not agree with the values of cultural liberalism, it is still defensive in the face of racism charges, and hence particularly vulnerable to those charges. Consequently, because of its moral weight, racism could be used to deconstruct the old society and help build a new one. By firing a constant barrage of racism charges at American society, liberals could weaken the defenses of social institutions and cultural values. If traditional values could be equated with the intolerance of racism, then those values would have to be discarded in favor of a new and "enlightened" tolerance that would in turn nurture new values, such as sexual freedom. If the whole web of cultural and moral values could be characterized as contributing to a mentality that had created and sanctioned black slavery, then the legitimacy of those values could be destroyed. And if the existing scheme of cultural and moral values could be destroyed, then a new cultural ideology could replace it—an ideology made up of the feminist, multiculturalist, relativist, and deconstructionist theories now infusing modern liberalism. Thus, race was seen as the cultural equivalent of the incendiary bombing of Dresden during World War II (which proved to be almost as destructive as the devastation seen at Hiroshima)—a complete eradication of the old.

In painting America as a racist country, liberals cast doubt on the credibility of America's moral standing during the cold war. If America was a racist country, then its claim to be protecting the democratic freedoms of the South Vietnamese was suspect. So too was its position vis-à-vis the Soviet Union. How could the United States claim moral superiority if it was infected with the immorality of racism? Race became the lens through which leftists could reveal the inherent evils of the American way of life. It became a direct rebuttal to all the flag-waving and Pledge-reciting and cold war patriotism of the 1950s. It became a tool with which to carry on an even larger campaign against everything bad about America—corporate greed, environmental pollution, sexism, moralism, religious bigotry. If America was wrong on race—and it had been—then America was also wrong on foreign policy, social welfare, and cultural values.

By 1972 the countercultural Left had become firmly established in the Democratic coalition. It not only saw America as no better than any other society or culture, it actually viewed America as having less moral authority than any other society or culture. Since America had done so many bad things (for example, racism), it would be wrong for anyone to embrace American cultural values. Consequently, moral authority should be transferred to all the international victims of America's imperialism.

The public career of John Kerry reflects the conflict between cultural liberalism and American moral legitimacy. After returning from Vietnam, Kerry joined the antiwar movement and proclaimed before a national television audience that American troops had committed systematic atrocities. Kerry called American soldiers indiscriminate killers and compared them to Genghis Khan. In testimony before the U.S. Senate, he said that Asians feared American "imperialism" more than communism. During the 1980s he argued that U.S. Central American policies violated international law and that President Ronald Reagan's support of the democratic Nicaraguan contras was damaging America's "moral credibility."[42] Kerry blamed the United States, not the Soviet Union, for the failure of arms-control talks in the early 1980s. He even condemned the 1983 U.S. liberation of Grenada as an unfair fight, saying that it represented a bully's show of force against a weak third-world nation. And at the 1988 Democratic convention, he characterized America as living in a time of "moral darkness."

This condemning-of-America liberalism remains alive and well in the modern Democratic Party. George Soros, the largest financial backer of the party, equated Bush's use of the Patriot Act to the way Nazi Germany and the Soviet Union preyed on their citizens and stifled dissent. He likened the prisoner abuse at Abu Ghraib to the attacks of 9/11.[43] Filmmaker Michael Moore, who became the ideological star of the Democratic Party in 2004, went so far as to blame America for the terrorist attacks of September 11; the attacks were the natural result of America's having previously been "culpable in committing so many acts of terror." Recognizing the prevalence of this victimization mind-set in his own party, Senator Evan Bayh (D-IN) acknowledged that the Democratic Party is often seen as "contemptuous" of the values by which most Americans live and proclaimed that Democrats "need to be a party that stands for more than the sum of our resentments."[44]

SEVEN

In *the* WakE of Race

THERE ARE two ways to kill weeds in a lawn. One is to use a specialized weed killer, sprayed directly on the particular weed to be killed. Another is to apply a general herbicide to the whole lawn. The latter approach is the easier and achieves the wider kill, but it will also destroy more than just the weeds. Choosing between the two options depends on one's priorities: killing the weeds or beautifying the lawn. With the former, the primary desire is to thicken the lush green grass by eliminating isolated patches of weeds. With the latter, the main desire is to get rid of the weeds, even if portions of the lawn die with them.

In the lawn of American society, racism charges have been routinely applied using the second approach. They have been sprayed the whole expanse of society rather than directed specifically to the roots of individual weeds. Consequently, much of the surrounding grass has been yellowed or even killed by the racism herbicide, and this overkill reflects the social priorities of the past several decades. America has been more concerned with getting rid of the weeds of racism than with strengthening the lush grass of society. As a result of this focus, an inverse relationship has evolved: the more racially sensitive America has become, the more coarse and harsh its culture has become. Ideally, the more racial justice a society achieves, the more culturally rich it should become. But because of the way in which racial politics have evolved in America, this has not been the result.

With racism charges being applied in the manner of a general herbicide across the whole lawn of society, the social grass has become stressed and weakened. And the more wilted and yellowed the grass becomes, the less the groundskeepers care about it, and the less they try to maintain it. Likewise, the more America is branded as racist, the more its citizens lose faith in their cultural values and social institutions. What Edmund Burke once said about revolutions—that they tend to devour their children and turn into their own opposites—now describes America's civil rights revolution. Whereas the civil rights movement was once about freedom and equality, it has now bred a politics of race that feeds on undefined guilt and irrational fear.

Racism has been in the public spotlight for at least four decades. This attention was long overdue, as were the reforms it brought. But the singular focus on eliminating racism has come to blind society from seeing certain cultural side effects. There has been so much attention paid to the disease that the patient has been ignored, although it makes no sense to cure a disease if the patient dies in the process.

The civil rights movement made an invaluable contribution to America. But this contribution has not come without a downside. Racism has been America's gravest wrong, and in seeking to make atonement, the nation has given a moral carte blanche to those representing the victims of racism. Hence, the crusade against racism has proceeded without any moral checks and balances, leaving the objects of its accusations defenseless. In addition, the antiracism cause has been used to promote agendas that go far beyond race.

Race has been the launching pad for the multicultural movement—a movement that seeks not just an end to racial discrimination, but a ripping out of the historical roots of American culture. The multicultural ideology essentially denies all Western claims to truth and represents "the deconstruction of the foundational ideals of Western civilization."[1] It stems from the premise that Western civilization is fundamentally racist because it elevates Eurocentric or "white" values over those of other cultures. Moreover, this "white culture" has prevailed only because it has suppressed all minority cultures; racism, and racism alone, explains why Western civilization is richer and more powerful than any third world culture. According to novelist Toni Morrison, oppression is what distinguishes Western civilization.[2] As Ishmael Reed writes, "It's because of Eurocentric control of the public school curriculum that the U.S. produces generation after generation of white bigots."[3]

In *The Rise of Radical Egalitarianism*, political scientist Aaron Wildavsky examines the impulses fueling multiculturalism, including the urge to regard all whites as oppressors and all minority groups as victims, to see America as incorrigibly racist, to politicize all academic disciplines, and to snuff out dissent. And all these impulses, according to Wildavsky, revolve around a different notion of egalitarianism—a belief in eliminating the differences among all people in society by setting the bar at a level where the victims are seen as the victors.

Perceiving Western culture as irrevocably corrupted by racism, sexism, colonialism, and imperialism, multicultural advocates look to other societies for an alternative to the oppressive institutions of white society. However, there is a double standard here: while other cultures are exempt from moral criticism, Western culture is singularly condemned as repugnant. Yet contrary to the pronouncements of the multiculturalists, the universal appeal of Western culture is evident in the tide of immigrants flooding into Europe and the United States, hoping to take advantage of Western prosperity and opportunity. If America is so racist, then why do so many new immigrants from so many different countries keep arriving?

In seeking to brand the West in as negative a light as possible, multicultural textbooks tell tales of the genocide done by white invaders on innocent natives, as in the diseases brought from Europe, but mention

131

nothing of the savagery and slavery of natives, including the practices of human sacrifice by the Aztecs and the cannibalism of the Incas. Furthermore, a close examination of many of the dominant cultures of Asia, Africa, and Latin America reveals that these cultures are not as conducive to democratic rule, equality, individual freedom, civic virtue, reason, and open commerce.

Despite its belief in cultural relativism—that no culture is any better than any other culture—multiculturalism singles out Western culture as an exception. Not only is it no better than any other culture, it is actually worse—it is somehow uniquely corrupt. Thus, by identifying America with colonialism and slavery, multiculturalists see it as inferior to the rest of the world, insofar as it is a place where the white majority oppresses the nonwhite disadvantaged.

This ideology is a direct attack on Martin Luther King Jr.'s vision of a multiracial society composed of free and equal races living harmoniously under the governance of America's Western-style cultural institutions. King wanted to bring blacks into a full participation in American culture; he did not want to break up that culture into "separate but equal" multicultures. He saw culture as distinct from race—a society could be composed of many races, but have only one culture. To King, the only way for different races to coexist was for them to live in a culture with shared understandings of the rights and obligations of citizens. Consequently, rather than rejecting the moral and cultural foundations of America, as the multiculturalists now do, King embraced them. He used the moral principles of the Bible Belt, for instance, to fight the evil of segregation that existed within that Bible Belt.

The open door was immediately apparent to anyone pushing his cart down the freezer aisle at the grocery store. The swinging glass door was almost four feet wide, and it stuck straight out into the aisle, forcing the passing carts into a sort of bottleneck. A child had climbed inside the freezer and was standing on the bottom shelf, bracing himself with one hand on the frame and holding open the door with the other. A foggy steam spilled out of the open door. But none of the passing shoppers said anything. They veered around the open door, squeezing up against the far side of the aisle, without showing even an acknowledgment of the child. A store clerk at the end of the aisle likewise feigned ignorance, focusing intently on the tubs of ice cream he was stacking.

Eventually, another door opened, and another, and yet another—each being held by a child who had climbed into a freezer compartment. Still nothing happened. Finally, a young woman—the mother of the first child to have climbed into the freezer—came around the corner and loudly scolded her child, commanding him to come out of the freezer and close the door. She was black, as was her child. Within seconds, the other mothers—all white—did likewise and pulled their children out from the freezers. The clerk at the end of the aisle was visibly relieved.

Both the multicultural and deconstructionist philosophies employ race to cast doubt on a wide array of traditional social values and institutions. The multicultural view uses race to attack the very foundations of Western civilization, characterizing them as inherently racist.[4] Consequently, everything from natural law to Judeo-Christian religious beliefs to democratic processes and individual freedom is discredited. Deconstructionists reduce everything to what they claim is the only true core of reality— power, oppression, and racism. The great treasures of art are seen not for their beauty, but as reflections of the oppressive and racist cultures that produced them. To the deconstructionists, modern art (such as the dung-studded Madonna and the urine-soaked crucifix) liberates society by stripping away all the false illusions of the past. The fact that the art is also dehumanizing and desolating only serves to elevate its "moral" message.

Ironically, in this time of terrorism, cultural leftists through their deconstructionist use of race have already done more to denigrate from within what Islamic terrorists seek to destroy from without—a culture based on the norms of Western civilization. For this reason, the war on terror is forcing America to rethink almost four decades of cultural liberalism and relativism; it is forcing America to either fight for its values and ideals in a civilizational war, or lose them.

In *Who Are We? The Challenge to America's National Identity*, Samuel Huntington documents the leftist assault on American culture. He argues that multiculturalists have dismissed the role that Anglo-Protestant cultural elements—such as Christianity, the rule of law, individual opportunity, and the work ethic—have played in America's history. Huntington also describes how, beginning in the 1960s, the cultural left launched a sustained effort—one that is "quite possibly without precedent in human history"—to undercut national identity and loyalty by eroding the foundations of America's common culture.[5] And at the forefront of that effort has been the battle for racial preferences, which contradict a core principle of the American creed: the concept of equal rights regardless of race.

This breakdown of national identity is particularly evident in the separatist movement going on in Hawaii. The goal of the movement is to establish a race-based governing entity for native Hawaiians that could eventually secede from the United States. Its popularity stands in stark contrast with public sentiments surrounding Hawaii's entry into the Union in 1959, when 94 percent of Hawaiians voted in favor of statehood. Today, however, with the arrival of multiculturalism and the Hawaiian-rights movement, the government does not even acknowledge Statehood Day. Moreover, an official state agency, the Office of Hawaiian Affairs, is dedicated to creating a separate Hawaiian nation; but because of fears of being called racist, few public officials dare criticize the documented and notorious wastefulness of the agency.[6]

The multicultural revolution against traditional values and institutions takes several forms. First, it seeks a replacement of individual identities and rights with group identities and rights. Second, it downplays majority rule as the primary mechanism of democratic government; according to multiculturalists, majority rule gives insufficient weight to minority or victim groups. Third, it deconstructs, and then reconstructs, the historical identity of America. Fourth, it denies that nations should comprise peoples united by a common culture, and it seeks to replace civic patriotism with a collection of narrow racial and ethnic loyalties.

A focus on victimhood characterizes this cultural revolution in America. By concentrating only on the wrongs America has caused, the victim mentality can be used to delegitimize mainstream social institutions and ideologies. By glorifying the victim, we condemn that which caused the victim—mainstream society. In seeing the victim as a kind of moral hero, we cast doubt on the moral integrity of a society that produced that victim. This is why cultural leftists cringe at any overt signs of patriotism, like the recitation of the Pledge of Allegiance. To them, even the mention of a singular national purpose prompts instinctive opposition, because any such expression would be viewed only from the standpoint of those individuals who might feel oppressed by such a show of national will. And again, race is a potent tool in this victimization crusade, since victims of racism are seen as the most innocent and sympathetic victims. Moreover, once a victim orientation is constructed on the foundation of race, it can expand out to encompass new categories of victims, including illegal aliens who claim to have just as much right to America and all its benefits as do U.S. citizens.

This victimized outlook, with its accusatory stance toward society and its institutions, was particularly evident during the hearings of the 9/11 Commission, where the villain behind the terrorist attacks became not the terrorists themselves but the U.S. government. The headlines of the hearings proclaimed: "9/11 Panel Faults U.S. Government."[7] Even the former New York City police and fire chiefs came under harsh criticism from the 9/11 Commission. Families of the 9/11 victims loudly applauded the Commission's tough and confrontive questioning of the chiefs, as well as of the government's intelligence and national security personnel. This was just the kind of blame-America-first attitude that Democrats displayed when they claimed that the Patriot Act was more repressive than the Taliban. It is the kind of victimized outlook that refuses to let law enforcement officials use profiling techniques as an investigative tool to identify terrorists, despite the tremendous threat that terrorism poses and despite the fact that evidence clearly shows that terrorists do have a profile: young adult, Muslim males, of Middle Eastern and North African descent.

Besides using race as a tool in weakening the hold of traditional moral and cultural values, liberals have employed race in an attack on the larger notion of American "specialness," as expressed by Ronald Reagan in his "City on a Hill" metaphor. This attack had initially started with the Vietnam War protests, which conveyed the message that America possessed no special righteousness, that it too was capable of violence and imperialism and oppression. America was in many ways a sick nation, the liberals preached. And its racism was the most vile symptom of that sickness.

Opponents of affirmative action decided to launch a Web site encouraging white college applicants to commit an act of civil disobedience by identifying themselves as minorities on their application forms. "Imagine," said one of the Web site organizers, "a dean standing at the front gate of the university, turning away a white student who had lied on her application." Or as another put it: "To what extent will admissions officers go to verify the race of an applicant?"

Unfortunately, America's racial politics has helped move the nation from an assimilation society toward an adversarial one. In lamenting the erosion of the assimilation model, James Bennett in *The Anglosphere Challenge: Why the English-speaking Nations Will Lead the Way in the Twenty-First Century* argues that "it is our core values and characteristics that have made us dynamic, and it is to those values that we must return." Under the assimilation model, society was seen as a collection of cooperating individuals who sacrifice their differences for the sake of social cohesion. As Samuel Huntington argues, this assimilation model prevailed until the late 1960s, encouraging the cultural absorption of immigrants, with each wave of previous immigrants conforming to the prevailing American cultural values. But an adversarial culture has abandoned any effort at commonality or consensus; it pushes individuals toward conflict, continually challenging community authority. An incident described by Huntington illustrates this point. At a Gold Cup soccer game between Mexico and the United States in February 1998, the 91,255 fans were immersed in a sea of red-white-and-green flags. They booed when "The Star-Spangled Banner" was played. They pelted the U.S. players with debris and threw things at fans who tried to raise an American flag. But the surprising fact was that the game took place not in Mexico City but in Los Angeles.

A similar scenario occurred during a March 25, 2006 march in Denver. In that march, more than fifty thousand people protested congressional legislation that would have made illegal immigration a felony. The point of the march was to stress the desire of illegal immigrants to become U.S. citizens and to claim their full legal and political rights under the American system. But the disconnect occurred when many of the marchers waved Mexican flags.

In an adversarial culture, the public is more oriented to the rights it can assert against government than what it might contribute toward a common good. Blacks turn against whites, demanding certain rights and entitlements. And then whites turn against each other or against the government, demanding their own set of rights. Everyone becomes adversarial to one another, and to society as a whole. A combative edge intensifies within society, as evidenced by all the incidents of road rage and outbursts of violence. In a country that once had "Have a Nice Day" as its national slogan, citizens now wear sweatshirts that scream "Back Off." Huge audiences watch reality television shows that thrive on rude and boorish acts of confrontation and backbiting.

A decline in civility reflects the growing contentiousness of American society. Symptomatic of this rising incivility, according to social scientist Elijah Anderson, is a growing urban oppositional culture.[8] The code of the nation's streets, argues Anderson, commands the youth to compete for respect and status by "dissing" or "messing with" each other. But this oppositional culture is not confined to the inner city.[9] It reverberates throughout all of American society. As Pete Hamill writes, American society "is becoming swept away by a poisonous floodtide of confrontation, vulgarity and flat-out, old-fashioned hatred."[10]

A large sign in a day-care center contained a list of rules regarding eating habits, music-listening, video-game-playing, and use of language. But it had to be taken down after a parent insisted on the enforcement of those rules.

One consequence of multiculturalism has been an attack on cultural standards and social behavioral norms. A prime example of how such norms have dissipated amid a deconstructed culture appears in the increasing chaos and violence attending American sporting events. As a microcosm of society, these sporting events reveal a stark decline in social obedience to behavioral standards.

On November 19, 2004, a brawl occurred during an NBA game between the Indiana Pacers and the Detroit Pistons. The fight first broke out among the players and then spread to the fans, who threw food and drinks onto the playing floor. Players then went into the stands and starting punching spectators. Pistons Coach Larry Brown said he had never seen anything like it.[11] The very next day, a huge fight broke out at the Clemson–South Carolina college football game. But these were just two of the most flagrant instances of uncontrolled behavior by fans and athletes. Several days after the Pacers-Pistons brawl, police had to use a stun gun to subdue a Minnesota Timberwolves basketball player who had repeatedly refused to leave a bar at closing time.[12]

In *Out of Bounds: Inside the NBA's Culture of Rape, Violence and Crime*, author Jeff Benedict states that 40 percent of U.S.-born NBA players have had criminal complaints filed against them. Even during their games, they taunt other players, yell obscenities at the referees, and throw temper tantrums on the sidelines—a stark contrast to the on-court dignity of an Oscar Robertson or Bill Russell thirty years ago. But what is truly remarkable is that, despite this foul behavior, society still treats these individuals as role models for youth.[13] Not surprisingly, youth sports have turned increasingly violent, and not only from the stand-point of the players. Dozens of state legislatures have passed laws impos-ing stiff penalties on fans and parents who abuse or attack sporting-event referees.[14] These laws have been necessitated by the thousands of referees who have left high school and youth sports in recent years because of abusive behavior on the part of spectators.

The decline of behavioral standards is further apparent in the after-math of any sports championship victory. Fans go out into the streets and riot—overturning cars, breaking storefront windows, and looting shops. This lawlessness is a perverse descendant from the urban riots of the 1960s—a lawlessness that results from decades of a cultural rela-tivism that ignores individual duty and moral behavior. And when these riots end in tragedy, as happened with the death of a young woman hit by police pepper spray after the Boston Red Sox won the 2004 Ameri-can League pennant, the blame goes to the police who were vainly try-ing to control a crowd of eighty thousand, not to the people who started the riot in the first place.

An even more serious problem resulting from a decline in behavioral standards occurs within the nation's schools. All evidence suggests that unruly student behavior is on the rise. In states like Ohio, Virginia, Ken-tucky, and Florida, juvenile court judges are complaining that they are being overwhelmed by student misconduct cases.[15] Furthermore, this mis-conduct appears to be skewed by race. In Toledo, even though minorities comprise less than 50 percent of the student body, they account for 65 percent of the safe-school violations. But herein lies a vicious circle: since racism is often alleged whenever minority children are disciplined, a re-laxation of behavioral standards brings an increasing tolerance of miscon-duct, which only increases the misconduct. Furthermore, since racism is often asserted against teachers and principals who try to discipline minority students, it is not surprising that behavioral problems are more common in schools located in minority neighborhoods.[16] The severity of student misconduct has even caused some school districts to call in the police and juvenile justice authorities. Toledo, for instance, has had dozens of students arrested for violating the city's safe-school ordinance.[17]

The horrible effect that a decline in behavioral standards has exerted on the most vulnerable members of society is illustrated in *Made in Detroit,* Paul Clemens's memoir of growing up in Detroit in the 1970s. Even at the age of ten, Clemens noticed that his black teammates on the football team had trouble making practice because their single, working mothers were unable to repair broken bicycle chains or drive their sons to the field. Many of those teammates also didn't seem to have permanent homes: "They just stay somewhere," Clemens tragically notes. He also recalls how his mostly white, mostly Catholic enclave—"notable, perhaps, less for its positive qualities than for its relative lack of negative ones: no abandoned homes, no broken-down cars, no broken-out windows"—became a Halloween night destination for black families seeking a safe place for their children to go trick-or-treating, away from the gunfire and arson. Indeed, Halloween night in Detroit singularly reflects the transformation that has occurred in social behavior. During the 1950s, children would engage in such benign pranks as ringing doorbells and running away; whereas by the 1980s, Detroit's teenagers had taken to arson, trying each year on Halloween night to burn their city down.

Tragically, this Halloween snapshot is mirrored every day of the year in a society where criminality is steadily increasing. In 1981, 0.9 percent of the population was under correctional supervision; but by 2003, the figure had risen to 2.4 percent.[18] Another indicator of unsocialized behavior is the refusal to work. In 1954, 9 percent of young black males were neither working nor looking for work; but by 1999, a year of very low unemployment, the figure had jumped to 30 percent. This trend correlates directly with the number of young men who have grown up without fathers. During the 1950s, the illegitimacy ratio in America was 4 percent; but by 2003, the ratio had increased to 35 percent, with the black illegitimacy rate at 68 percent.[19]

Even though the 1990s had the best labor market in three decades, black men were not able to take advantage of it. Contrary to the progress made by black women and Hispanic men, black men saw their unemployment and incarceration rates continue to rise.[20] By 2004, 72 percent of black male high school dropouts in their twenties were jobless, compared with 19 percent of Hispanic dropouts.[21] Among black dropouts in their late twenties, "more are in prison on a given day—34 percent—than are working—30 percent."[22]

BY MAKING race the exclusive moral value, the multiculturalists have effectively downgraded all preexisting moral values. One implication of this can be seen in the dominant influence of diversity in the corporate world. Former CEOs, known for their ruthless and ethically challenged corporate leadership, take up residence at nonprofit foundations where they sponsor conferences on corporate diversity and give awards for innovative diversity programs. It is as if the mere pursuit of the cause of diversity suddenly transforms these ex-CEOs from a Mr. Potter to a George Bailey, as if it suddenly cleanses a ruthless and hard-hearted past—as if none of their previous business sins matter, now that they publicly proclaim the need for diversity.

But there is a problem when a corporation's diversity accomplishments become the only measure of that corporation's ethical or moral conduct. All attention is placed on what a corporate workforce looks like, not on what it is doing. This kind of indifference created the conditions in which WorldCom and Enron were able to carry out their fraudulent financial schemes on such a mammoth scale. As David Callahan reveals in *The Cheating Culture: Why More Americans Are Doing Wrong to Get Ahead*, corporate crime escalated throughout the 1990s—during a time when most of society's attention was focused on whether corporations were achieving the necessary racial diversity. This does not mean that racism is less serious than financial fraud, only that it should not blind society to the dangers and occurrences of such fraud. Corporations spend hundreds of millions of dollars hosting diversity seminars and hiring diversity consultants, but they spend minute fractions of that on moral ethics courses.

There came a point in time when the crusade against racism came to be waged within a larger culture of moral erosion. Social chronicler Tom Wolfe captures this culture in his most recent novel, *I Am Charlotte Simmons*. In that novel, a young woman leaves a small town and enters an elite university. There, she finds all the rules of life have disappeared—the rules of courtship, virtue, and even decorum. Those rules are gone because the morality that once supported them has disappeared. As Wolfe points out, the word *immoral* now seems almost obsolete. But the multicultural movement's rejection of traditional moral values has had particularly harmful effects on the youth. Sixty percent of all gonorrhea cases occur in the age group fifteen to twenty-four, according to the Alan Guttmacher Institute. Children in single-parent families are three times as likely as children in two-parent families to have emotional and behavioral problems.[23] Black children in single-parent homes have significantly lower achievement scores than those in two-parent homes.[24] Indeed, family life, rather than race, appears to be the determinant of poverty. Black children raised by married couples are almost as unlikely to be poor as are whites raised in the same manner.[25] Despite these facts, however, multiculturalists theorize that single parenthood is just another, perfectly desirable alternative lifestyle. They claim that black female–headed households constitute "meaningful and productive lifestyles that do not conform to white societal norms."[26] As Alice Walker argues, the Western tradition of marriage is obsolete.[27]

The assault on cultural codes and values has also spilled over to such "value-free" standards as those relating to academic and intellectual pursuits. Reflecting an "anything-goes" approach, schools in Oakland,

California actually teach the speaking of Ebonics.[28] This is because among many black youths, the use of standard English and academic achievement is demeaned as "acting white."[29] When the *Wall Street Journal* profiled Cedric Jennings, an accomplished high school student in Washington, D.C., Jennings admitted that he had been regularly insulted by other black students who looked on him as a racial apostate. "The charge of wanting to be white, where I'm from, is like treason," Jennings said.[30]

Throughout the field of education, and similar to the effects of cultural relativism elsewhere in society, rigorous enforcement of academic standards has given way to a focus on the self-esteem of the lowest performing students. In *Hard America, Soft America,* Michael Barone discusses how schools have abandoned the hard rigors of intellectual excellence in favor of fostering students' self-esteem. Instead of teaching them to compete and rewarding the achievements of that competition, schools focus on a one-sided lesson of racial discrimination—an indiscriminate tolerance of everyone and everything, regardless of performance. In *A Nation Deceived: How Schools Hold Back America's Brightest Students,* the John Templeton Foundation reveals how the education system inhibits and restrains gifted students so as not to stigmatize the other students. This stigma concern is a direct offshoot of the arguments used in racial discrimination cases—the argument against any policy that would in any way suggest that any singular group of people is not equal in all respects to every other group.

The relativistic ambiguity spawned by the multicultural movement has come to extend far beyond matters of race and morals. It has contributed to an erosion of educational demands and expectations. One poll reveals that while 90 percent of Ivy League students could identify Rosa Parks, only 25 percent could name the author of the words "government of the people, by the people, for the people."[31] In another survey, 40 percent of seniors at the nation's top colleges could not say within a half century when the Civil War was fought. And more high school students knew who Harriet Tubman was than knew that Washington commanded the American army during the Revolutionary War.[32]

Even such objective rules as those governing grammar have lost their edge. In *I'm the Teacher, You're the Student*, Emory University historian Patrick Allitt writes that few of his students are familiar with the basic rules of the English language. American students are also drifting away from the hard sciences requiring mastery of objective knowledge and toward the softer disciplines whose "truths" can often be subjectively washed away into a relativistic position of "every answer is as good as the next." From 1975 to 2004, the United States fell in its proportion of college students majoring in science and engineering from third in the world to seventeenth, and in 2003, 75 percent of the Intel Science Talent Search finalists were immigrants.[33]

The merit system has similarly come under attack. Whenever they fail to produce the results dictated by proportional representation, merit standards are seen as a racist ploy of the dominant culture. Even standardized testing has been branded as racist. "Any tests that emphasize logical, analytic methods of problem-solving will be biased against minorities," says an official of the Atlanta public school system.[34] Standardized tests, according to Richard Seymour of the Lawyers' Committee for Civil Rights, are an "engine for the exclusion of minorities."[35]

When the Chicago Police Department announced the results of its 1994 sergeant test, only 8 percent of the five hundred officers who scored high enough to win promotion were African American. Protests immediately came from black leaders who said the test was racially biased, but just a few years earlier Chicago had paid more than five million dollars to several consulting firms to devise multiple-choice tests that were free of bias. Moreover, Asians who took the test scored higher than whites, undermining charges that the test simply measured familiarity with white middle-class norms.[36]

Contrary to the arguments of discrimination, numerous studies examining black and white academic performance have concluded that standardized IQ tests are not biased against African Americans.[37] Indeed, blacks do worse on IQ tests than Eskimos and immigrants from Far Eastern countries, whose ways of life are far more distant from white middle-class norms in America.[38] Some researchers have even found that standardized tests such as the SAT are actually biased in favor of blacks.[39]

As with the opposition to testing, there is a similar move to abolish certain job requirements that might inhibit minority advancement. The State Department, upon discovering that few African Americans speak foreign languages, frequently discards that requirement in its efforts to increase minority representation; and since 1979, it has used a "near pass" category so that blacks who fail the entrance exam can still be considered for jobs.[40] In the private sector, companies have been sued merely for requiring that employees have a high school diploma or that they not have a criminal record. These standards amount to racial discrimination, according to the plaintiffs, because blacks are less likely to graduate from school and more likely to be convicted of a crime than whites.[41] Some activists even propose forcing companies to change their job descriptions or eliminate job requirements altogether so that more blacks can meet the new requirements.[42] Others argue that companies should be forced to develop new kinds of businesses in which African Americans would be more comfortable.[43]

A Nobel Prize–winning novelist once said, "Find me the Tolstoy of the Zulus, or the Proust of the Papuans, and I would be happy to read him." He was immediately accused of racism, even though he did not say that the Zulus or the Papuans were incapable of producing great novelists, just that they had not yet done so.

Cultural relativism is a uniquely Western ideology. No Muslim thinks that Allah's teachings are simply relativistic notions that are true for some people but not for everyone. Only in Western cultures, where the tradition of free speech and individualism prevails, is there cultural relativism. But this obviously leaves the West in general and America in particular at a disadvantage in relation to other cultures.[44] As an American professor proclaims in condemning his own society, "U.S. patriotism is inseparable from . . . white supremacy."[45] The philosopher Martha Nussbaum argues that "patriotic pride" is "morally danger-ous."[46] New York University's Richard Sennett condemns "the evil of a shared national identity. And Cecilia O'Leary of American University describes patriotism as a right-wing, militaristic, repressive force.

During the peace and prosperity years of the 1990s, when multicul-turalism rose to prominence within academia and liberal politics, there was little perceived need to defend American cultural values and institu-tions. But after September 11, 2001, and the ensuing war on terror, a cul-tural defense has become more necessary and urgent, because underlying the war on terror is a much larger conflict between Western democratic ideals and Islamic fanaticism. Aside from the war on terror, however, there are other indications of a need to defend traditional Western cul-ture. In the 2004 elections, voters registered a strong protest of moral rel-ativism. In a national exit poll conducted for the Associated Press and the major television networks, voters were asked to identify the issue that mattered most in their vote for president. "Moral values" topped the list, above even that of the economy and terrorism.[47]

As Rudyard Kipling believed, civilization is something laboriously achieved yet only precariously defended. And the war on terror has shown America just how much it needs to defend its Western traditions and values, as much from within as from without. Racism has to be fought whenever it appears, but only within the context of keeping Western culture strong. This has been a lesson learned in the Nether-lands, in the wake of Dutch filmmaker Theo van Gogh's murder by an Islamist extremist on November 2, 2004. Prior to that incident, the fa-mously tolerant and multicultural Dutch tended to look on any social conflict with Muslim extremism as a sign of Western intolerance and racism. They eagerly tolerated the disdain with which their growing

Muslim population treated Dutch freedoms.[48] However, after the van Gogh murder, even the liberal media did an about-face and called for a public crackdown on extremist Muslim fanatics, including the suppression of magazines and newspapers inciting Islamic violence.[49] The Dutch reversed their politically correct multicultural policies that sheltered radicalism. Attempts have been made to reduce the separateness of the Muslim community. But as Francis Fukayama notes, lying ahead is the more difficult problem "of fashioning a national identity that will connect citizens of all religious and ethnicities in a common democratic culture."[50]

At the same time that the Netherlands was getting its wake-up call on Islamic extremism, the Germans were also receiving a revelation. A German television station had secretly placed a camera inside an Islamic Mosque. This camera recorded the Imam saying: "Their [the Germans'] sweat spreads evil smells; they stink; they are atheists. . . . What good do they do us? They can only burn in hell."[51] Another revelation came by way of a publicly read letter from a Muslim living in Germany, stating that it was "outrageous that Germans demand we speak their language; our children will have our language, our laws, our culture." In response, Christian Democratic leader Joerg Schoenbohm proclaimed: "Those who come here have to adopt the German culture; our history has developed over a thousand years; we cannot allow that this basis of our commonality be destroyed by foreigners."

The November 2005 rioting of Arab youths in the suburbs of Paris provided further evidence of the challenges posed by Muslim radicalism to Western societies. Those riots came as a shock to France's self-image as a model of tolerance and multiculturalism. Indeed, "no country in the West has done more to cultivate world Arab opinion, to appease Arab terrorists, to ostentatiously oppose American Middle East policy" than France.[52] What the rioting revealed, however, was the risks of multiculturalism—what happens when ethnic communities can exclude themselves from the broad currents of national life. It revealed how multiculturalism weakens the social bonds of the community, how by removing any obligation to abide by the norms of the majority it condemns "whole sub-populations to the status of permanent second-class citizens."[53] Moreover, by removing any such obligations to adopt common national values, multiculturalism fosters a "values vacuum that breeds anomie and the pathologies of nihilism."[54]

Some critics claim that the British approach to race relations has fostered even more disunity and racial tensions than the French approach.[55] Instead of trying to assimilate its new immigrants into a cohesive national identity, Britain has employed a multicultural strategy that encourages immigrants to retain their ethnic and cultural differences. For instance, the government now provides separate schools for Muslims. Even in the non-Muslim public schools, British Muslim teenagers have the right to dress in full Islamic attire. Elsewhere, government officials have stated that prison wardens should not wear pins decorated with the English national flag, containing the red cross of St. George, since such pins might be seen as a racist symbol. Given such examples of self-denigrating racial appeasement, critics claim that "Britain is fast replacing nationhood with a hierarchy of victimhood, with different ethnic groups living in conflict, each trumpeting its own sense of grievance."[56]

ASIDE FROM the war on terror, the illegal immigration crisis presents yet another cultural challenge to America. However, the constant specter of racism charges has substantially weakened the nation's ability to address this challenge. Although a 2004 ballot initiative in Arizona, labeled Proposition 200, strove to enforce existing laws barring illegal immigrants from voting or receiving welfare benefits, it was vilified as racist. When a specially trained team of immigration agents apprehended 450 illegal aliens in several Southern California cities, the *Los Angeles Times* and various advocacy groups claimed that the arrests were racially motivated. The White House immediately suspended the team's work.[57] But this only prompted observers to note that the "fear of offending the race and rights lobbies has trumped national security at the Department of Homeland Security."[58]

Despite the often inflammatory debate about illegal immigration, America has shown throughout its history that it can absorb large numbers of immigrants. However, that previous absorption also coincided with policies that encouraged assimilation over separateness. There has never been a society that has absorbed unlimited diversity with limited commonality. To say that only diversity unites Americans is to say that nothing unites Americans. Just as every other nation and culture has done throughout history, Americans are entitled to preserve their way of life in the face of social challenges posed by illegal immigration. An undefined and unconstrained guilt over racism, however, threatens America with the loss of all positive aspects of Western culture, of which there is much to be proud.

The Greeks viewed civilization as a fragile creation that could not be taken for granted. Eighteenth-century philosophers and political theorists believed that civilized people could only be held together by a common culture, with accepted values and respected institutions. This culture could not be maintained through a cultural relativism that eroded all rules and codes of conduct, but by an adherence to the high standards of democratic citizenship. In modern America, however, the multiculturalists' attack on traditional civilizational standards has spawned much antisocial and destructive behavior—and this is not just a minority problem but a national problem.

The moral retreat caused by relativism is often described as a desire not to blame the victim. Consequently, the focus falls only on the perceived oppressor, as if the victim did not exist as an independent actor. But victims are not moral purities, immune from any criticism. A sympathy for victims should not be confused with the virtue of victims; nor should a culture of relativism be allowed to subvert a culture of decency.

EIGHT

The Shackles of GuiLt

ALTHOUGH RACE has become the defining cultural morality issue, it has simultaneously prompted a moral retreat within society. Because racism lacks the objective definition it once had, it infuses society with doubt and anxiety. Because individuals do not know when or how they might be accused of racism, they refrain from voicing opinions not only on racial matters but on any other moral issue that might somehow have a racial dimension. Consequently, moral relativism becomes the only logical option.

In addition, all the social guilt and anxiety on race casts doubt on the moral credibility of democratic society, which in turn erodes the authority and effectiveness of democratic institutions. As a result, America has turned increasingly to the courts for guidance on public policy. Doubting the moral wisdom of its legislatures, America not only acquiesces in a more expansive role for the courts, it demands such an activist role.

The real danger posed by the racial climate in America is not that the races will ultimately fail to live together in harmony; the real danger goes far beyond the matter of race relations—it goes to the moral identity of society as a whole. The danger is that the current climate of racial politics will contribute to a moral gutting of society and that America will go the direction of France and Germany insofar as those countries allowed the big injustices of their past to leave them morally paralyzed in the present.

Following World War II, Germany not only had to recover from the physical devastations of war, it had to deal with the moral guilt of Nazism. France likewise had to live with the legacy of Vichy and its complicity with the Nazis. As historian Tony Judt reveals in *Postwar: A History of Europe Since 1945*, France not only acquiesced to the Nazi occupation, it often assisted in it. Indeed, this assistance was vital to the occupation, because only fifteen hundred Nazis and six thousand German policemen were assigned to govern France, a country of forty million people. Even after the war ended, France failed to fully own up to its complicity. According to Judt, 6,763 people were sentenced to death by French courts immediately after the war (though none for "crimes against humanity"), but only 791 were actually executed.

Both France and Germany have let the guilt of their World War II legacies erode their moral standing not only in the international arena but also at home. Throughout the postwar period, the two nations have steadily turned away from their traditional ties to moral authority. This turning away, according to George Weigel in *The Cube and the Cathedral: Europe, America, and Politics Without God*, has coincided with an increasing rejection of religion—a rejection exemplified by the decision to omit from the European Union's seventy-thousand-word constitution any reference to Europe's Christian heritage or influence. As Weigel argues, this omission reflects Europe's abandonment of a morally inspired democratic society in favor of a procedurally legalistic one. Weigel also argues that France and Germany's current demographic and cultural barrenness results from a rejection of its longstanding moral and cultural foundations.

Once very religious societies, France and Germany have become overwhelmingly secular. In France, only one in twenty people attends a religious service on a weekly basis, and only 10 percent believe religion to be "very important" in their lives.[1] In Germany, fewer than 15 percent attend church at least once a month.[2] By contrast, more than 60 percent of Americans claim that religion plays a "very important" role in their lives, and almost 90 percent profess a belief in God.[3] Although some 62 percent of Americans believe in a personal God, only a third of Europeans do.[4] Moreover, public opinion experts note that moral relativism is "predominant in Europe."[5] People in Europe are "embarrassed to talk about moral values," says Tessa Keswick of the Center for Policy Studies in London.[6] They have largely abandoned the fundamental values of the Western, Judeo-Christian tradition.[7]

The ways in which France and Germany commemorate World War II are indicative of the moral guilt that plagues those countries. (Indeed, France opposed its own Nazi occupation in 1940 with seemingly less vigor than it did the deposing of Saddam Hussein in 2003.) Their war museums, for instance, preach single-mindedly against the follies of war, regardless of the cause of that conflict or the aims of the combatants; all violence is decried, as if the Allied forces were just as culpable as the Nazi war machine. Only at the American and British cemeteries is a different vision of the war presented. There, the story of a defeat of an evil tyrant is told. Words like *courage, sacrifice,* and *duty* are chiseled above the granite pavilions. But those words are never used in Germany or France—two countries who had to rely on outsiders to purge the Nazi virus from their borders; two countries that have lapsed into moral relativism because they have never found a way to resolve the moral guilt of their past. Instead of assuming responsibility for its Vichy past, France continues to blame certain victimizing social forces that left it vulnerable to Nazi exploitation—forces like racism, militarism, capitalism, and Western values.

France and Germany's moral impotence can also be seen in their paralysis in the face of modern crises, such as the genocide in Sudan, the nuclearization of Iran, and the secretive arms dealings with Iraq during the years of U.N. sanctions. This moral impotence has fostered a culture of "defeatism and appeasement."[8] It is an appeasement that has shown itself in the almost unconditional support given to dictators like Saddam Hussein and Yasser Arafat. As a noted Harvard historian has observed, "Many Europeans have behaved as if the optimal response to the growing threat of Islamist terrorism is to distance Europe from the United States."[9]

Although the current moral malaise of France and Germany can be traced to an unresolved guilt those nations feel over a great wrong in their past, there is a big difference in the way France and Germany handled their "big wrong" and the way America has dealt with its "big wrong"—the difference being that America addressed that wrong itself. During a four-year civil war, nearly three-quarters of a million soldiers died in the struggle to end slavery—and this does not count the wounded, the maimed, and the families who were left destitute because the war had taken their homes, their property, and their breadwinners. A century later, America underwent a tumultuous civil rights movement that combated segregation and racial injustice. Congress passed new laws; states reshaped their educational systems; and neighborhoods and communities examined and debated their racial attitudes and practices.

America has been struggling for a century and a half to rectify the wrong of slavery, but a necessary step in rectifying this wrong is to confront the social guilt over slavery. Guilt can gag a society's moral voice; and guilt regarding something as powerful as racism can impose a moral silencing on issues that stretch far beyond race. The challenge, obviously, is to avoid becoming morally helpless because of lingering guilt over the sins of the past.

Resolving racial guilt is a duty that whites must undertake with courage and conviction—the courage to honestly assess one's racist proclivities, and the conviction to stand by whatever that assessment yields.

Most racial policies, like affirmative action, play in some way to a silent and fearful white guilt. But in terms of feeding off guilt, nothing can rival the reparations movement.

During every congressional session since 1989, Representative John Conyers Jr. (D-MI) has introduced a bill mandating the payment of reparations for slavery.[10] Although the bill has never received a committee hearing, it has been steadily gathering strength, particularly among Democrats.[11] In 2000, the party's platform statement called for the establishment of a federal commission to make recommendations concerning the payment of reparations. During a campaign rally in Tulsa, Oklahoma, Al Gore said that reparations were "a definite possibility."[12] Even the Democratic governor of Michigan, Jennifer Granholm, has given her support to reparations and to Conyers's bill.[13]

As a first step toward reparations, various states and localities have passed laws requiring corporations to produce any business records showing that they or their corporate predecessors profited in any way from the slave trade in America. In May 2002, Governor Gray Davis of California backed a state law requiring insurance companies to disclose if they or their predecessors had ever issued policies to slaveholders.[14] Later that year, the Chicago City Council passed an ordinance requiring contractors to produce documents showing whether they may have had any economic connection to slavery.[15] In 2003, both the Los Angeles and Detroit City Councils approved legislation mandating businesses seeking city contracts to disclose any profits once made from slavery.[16] However, the venue in which the reparations movement has been gaining the most ground has been the courts. In March 2002, for instance, a suit against the Aetna Insurance Company, FleetBoston Financial Corporation, and CSX Corporation was filed in New York federal court seeking payment of reparations for the descendants of slaves.[17] The lawsuit sought damages in the amount of $1.4 trillion—a figure roughly equal to the total amount of income taxes collected by the federal government each year. Another reparations-style lawsuit sought retribution from the state of Oklahoma and the city of Tulsa for damages incurred during the city's 1921 race riot.

The payment of reparations obviously poses monumental problems. It would open up a Pandora's box of other groups seeking reparations for the injustices suffered by their ancestors. Irish and Chinese immigrants, for instance, faced institutionalized discrimination as well as living conditions that were often worse than those experienced by black slaves. According to one historian, nearly half of the original colonists came to America not of their own free will but as indentured servants or white slaves.[18] An additional problem with reparations is that a growing number of black Americans do not have ancestors who were U.S. slaves.[19]

Reparations also ignore the prominent role that Africa played in the slave trade. It was Africans who first took slaves into captivity, selling them to European traders.[20] In fact, when the Europeans attempted to abolish slavery, some of the stiffest resistance came from African tribes.[21] If not for the enlightened ideas of the Europeans, Africa would have continued the slave trade; indeed, slavery still exists in parts of Africa, with perhaps the worst abuser being Sudan.

Another drawback to reparations, besides of course its sheer cost, is that many modern-day problems experienced by African Americans are not the result of slavery. For instance, in the early 1900s, when slavery was obviously a much more recent phenomenon than it is today, black illegitimacy was a fraction of what it is now. According to economist Walter Williams, 75 percent of black children during the early 1900s lived in two-parent households.[22] And in New York City, the figure was 85 percent, compared with less than 40 percent today. The crime rate was also lower, with black communities in the early twentieth century much safer than they are today. Indeed, many of the current conditions of inner-city blacks are more likely traced to the Great Society programs of the 1960s, which hooked blacks on welfare and crowded them into drug-infested high-rise tenements, than to the effects of slavery; or, as Thomas Sowell argues in *Black Rednecks and White Liberals*, the dysfunctional aspects of urban black culture are a legacy not of slavery but of Southern "cracker" culture.

Even if reparations were paid, there is no guarantee that racial harmony would suddenly ensue. History has shown that social and economic policies like welfare and affirmative action have done little to tone down the rhetoric of racial division. In a recent ruling, for example, a federal judge ordered the Boston Police Department to end its thirty-year-old affirmative action hiring program. According to the judge, there was no longer any need for the program.[23] But the fact that minorities were now fully represented in the Boston Police Department prompted no statement of accomplishment by civil rights activists.

Despite all the arguments against reparations, however, perhaps there is one to be made in their favor. Perhaps only some drastic and horrendously costly penalty can take away the racial guilt that white society feels. Perhaps reparations should be seen from a moral standpoint—as the only way to unshackle society's moral voice from the bonds of guilt.

Maybe it will have to take something truly drastic like reparations to finally do away with the destructive effects of racial preferences.[24] (Most likely, however, reparations would have an even more divisive legacy than affirmative action has had: it would not only fail to achieve racial harmony, but would actually intensify racial suspicions and hostilities.) First, racial preferences can undermine blacks' incentives to strengthen their competitive abilities, since employers and teachers who fear that blacks cannot meet expected standards often respond by lowering those standards, which in turn encourage blacks to perform at the lowered standards.[25] Second, racial preferences tend to create an institutionalized view of blacks as presumptively disadvantaged on account of their race. Third, racial preference programs have made blacks dependent on the state. Indeed, some black leaders say that it was the government welfare programs that doomed black businesses: "Socialism destroyed the black community," claims black urban developer Don Scoggins. "We went where the money was, and that was in the welfare state."[26] And finally, affirmative action programs have been found to actually hurt minorities. As several researchers have demonstrated, placing minorities in schools that demand a performance level beyond that which those minorities are prepared to meet has led to disproportionately high dropout rates.[27]

According to a recent study by Professor Richard Sander published in the *Stanford Law Review,* racial preferences in law school admissions "produces more harms than benefits" to black applicants and law students.[28] As a result of these preferences, "Most black law applicants end up at schools where they will struggle academically and fail at higher rates than they would in the absence of preferences."[29] Affirmative action, Sander argues, "hurts the group it is most designed to help" because it ends up "producing fewer black lawyers each year than would be produced by a race-blind system."[30] Only 43 percent of the black students starting law school ever become lawyers.[31] According to Sander, "Blacks as a whole would be unambiguously better off in a system without any racial preferences at all than they are under the current regime."[32] He argues that the elimination of racial preferences would enable black students to attend schools where they are more competitive with other students, in turn enabling black students to perform better and receive higher grades, which in turn would produce higher graduation rates and bar exam passage rates.

The adverse effects of affirmative action extend beyond just the academic performance of minorities; they also exert a distorting influence on the whole educational environment. As John McWhorter reports, a black college admissions officer stated that she mistrusted black applicants who did not need preferences, since they would "not be committed" to the university's black community.[33] Moreover, the experiences in Texas and California reveal the fallacy that black students can only succeed with preferences. After racial preferences were eliminated at the University of Texas in 1996, the number of black freshman actually increased by nearly 10 percent.[34] And after the banning of racial preferences in California, there was a 350 percent rise in the number of black high school students taking calculus as a college preparatory course.[35]

But if affirmative action admissions policies are as dubious as the evidence suggests, the question arises as to why academia is so intensely enthralled with them. The inescapable answer is that they exist not so much to help minority students as to provide racial cover for schools worried about their "diversity quotient." In the current academic environment, racial diversity has become the overriding standard by which faculty and administrators judge themselves and their institutions, and affirmative action supplies a comfortable and secure means of achieving this diversity. Thus, regardless of its effect on students, affirmative action provides academia a means by which to proclaim its racial virtue.

Indeed, there is little evidence that the type of racial preference/diversity message preached for decades by academia is having any real positive effect on students. A survey by Stanley Rothman and Seymour Martin Lipset shows that the more racial diversity is emphasized on a college campus, the less enthusiastic students are about the quality of education at that campus.[36] Rothman and Lipset also found that such diversity-focused schools actually experienced more reports of discrimination, not less. Similarly, in its annual nationwide survey of college freshmen, UCLA found that less than 30 percent considered "helping to promote racial understanding" to be an important personal goal. This was the lowest percentage since UCLA began doing the survey.[37] And while surveys show that 90 percent of law students agree that "having students of different races and ethnicities" constitutes a positive aspect of their educational experience, 40 percent stated that they rarely or never studied with people of different racial backgrounds.[38] Furthermore, in *America in Black and White: One Nation, Indivisible,* Abigail and Stephan Thernstrom amass mounds of data showing that the growth of the black middle class has not, as is commonly thought, been largely dependent on affirmative action. The Thernstroms also argue that race relations have improved more than proponents of race preferences acknowledge, and that they improved faster before the affirmative-action era.

Fundamentally, affirmative action is based on the same racial approach as the segregation policies against which Martin Luther King Jr. fought. In both instances, the government treats blacks as an inferior group totally controlled by the dictates of external forces. They are not seen as individuals, capable of making their own way and setting their own destiny.[39] An end to affirmative action, therefore, may give blacks a greater control over their own fate and let them break free of any addiction to preferences. And if the only way to do this, as well as end white guilt and remove the moral gag imposed by such guilt, is through some kind of reparations payment, then perhaps it should be explored. Even though reparations would obviously pose a dangerous threat to the social fabric—through the animosity and resentment engendered among the social groups denied any reparations for the past, or present, wrongs done to them or their ancestors—perhaps it is the only way to end the manipulative exploitation of the rhetoric of victimhood by giving society a concrete way of achieving absolution for past wrongs. As Debra Dickerson writes in *The End of Blackness*, "Blacks simply do not know who and how to be absent oppression—to cease invoking racism and reveling in its continuance is to lose the power to haunt whites."

One reason Conyers's reparation proposal has never attracted enough support to even garner a committee hearing is because it would bankrupt the U.S. Treasury. But if the payment of reparations is the only way for America to regain some sense of moral virtue, if it is the only way to unshackle the nation's moral voice on all the issues on which it has become so silent, then perhaps reparations is a price that has to be paid. The country can probably recover from economic bankruptcy—the Great Depression proved that—but it cannot recover from moral bankruptcy.

Reparations might not even be as expensive as many estimate. Since it would obviously replace affirmative action, it would save the high costs of those programs, as well as the escalating costs of racial discrimination litigation. In settling a racial discrimination lawsuit in 2000, for instance, Coca Cola agreed to spend nearly $1 billion on various diversity programs and campaigns. But the costs of affirmative action are even greater. A study conducted in 1991 found that affirmative action's direct and indirect costs were about $115 billion, with additional opportunity costs of $236 billion and a lowering of the gross national product of about 4 percent.[40]

Aside from the financial costs, a system of racial preferences imposes a smothering blanket of often petty and pointless rules. For instance, defensive over the low number of black head coaches, the National Football League instituted a rule requiring that when a team has a head-coaching vacancy it must interview at least one minority candidate. Consequently, the Detroit Lions team was fined two hundred thousand dollars in 2003 when it hired a new coach without interviewing any minority candidates; but the problem was, all the minority candidates contacted by the team declined to be interviewed.[41] Nonetheless, the Detroit City Council still passed a resolution condemning the hiring of Steve Mariucci, which led the president of the team to recite an apologetic litany of "I'm not a racist" proclamations, including the standard, "Some of my best friends are black."[42] Even the owner of the team, Bill Ford, felt compelled to chime in, pointing out that he had once been named NAACP Man of the Year.

Carl's aunt lived in a retirement community. She was always a card-player, and now she spent her time playing bridge with her neighbors. One day, en route to a meeting, Carl stopped in to see her, to drop off some batteries she had asked him to get for her. He was with a colleague from work. Carl told the colleague that it would be just a moment, that he could wait in the car—but the colleague wanted to come in. As the two men walked down the long hall toward the cafeteria table at which Carl's aunt and her friends were seated, Carl heard his colleague mutter: "All nice and white, I see; they'd probably kick me out if they didn't think I was the janitor."

Carl didn't know for sure if his colleague was joking; but he wanted to think so, because he didn't want to have to answer him. Carl was afraid of being associated with racism.

The issue of reparations is usually viewed from the perspective of black victimization. This is the same one-way perspective from which all attitudes on race are usually viewed. But perhaps reparations should be seen from the vantage point of the nonminority. Perhaps reparations should be viewed from the standpoint of trying to cleanse the ubiquitous and undefined racial guilt that haunts nonminorities.

It is this pervasive guilt and its silencing effects that have had such a corrosive influence on social morality. Bill Cosby addressed these influences when he stood up and voiced a lonely and often unarticulated position—lambasting young men in Baltimore for "knocking up" as many as half a dozen girls; criticizing single mothers in Atlanta for having sex within their children's hearing and then several days later bringing home a different man.[43] Indeed, the current state of opinion on race—for example, the acquiescence in a blanket indictment of all nonminorities—is not only failing to produce a more harmonious racial environment, but is actually spawning new kinds of prejudice and discrimination. A sixteen-year-old Hispanic girl is accused of "acting white" just because she excels in school; she gets teased for using "SAT words" when she's out with her friends.[44] A black student who pursues scholarly achievement is "jumped after school for answering too many questions" in the classroom; as one of his assaulters said, "Dude, you're whiter than they [whites] are."[45] But this rebellion against perceived "white" culture only harms minorities. It tells them that they have to think and act a certain way, that educational accomplishments are not part of their culture, that the rebellious and antisocial street culture is their only means of identity.

The manipulation of racial anger and the exploitation of racial guilt benefit no one except the civil rights establishment. At some point, all the trumped-up anger and guilt have to end. The slate has to be wiped clean. If reparations are the only way to do that, hence allowing society to return to a more vigorous moral life, then so be it.

America's ever-burgeoning and unconstrained antidiscrimination crusade now threatens to inflict a grave injury on American society. It has already drained the country of any sense of cultural confidence, any belief in the enduring strength of its cultural values and institutions. The antidiscrimination crusade has moved beyond combating occurrences of racial injustice and has become a means of discrediting American culture in general, eroding its moral authority. And because of this erosion, just about any foreign alternative is seen to have a superior moral voice. Just about any foreign culture or government is considered more legitimate than America-the-victimizer. But only through a sense of cultural confidence can Americans truly protect their nation from all the forces so relentlessly threatening it. Only with such confidence can America move beyond the straitjacket of its apologetic defensiveness to the articulation of a unified moral mission.

ConclusiOn

IN TODAY'S discrimination mind-set, it is automatically assumed that anything done to any racial minority is the result of racial animosity. To even offer an alternative explanation is to risk being described as an apologist for racism. But Michelle Malkin's *In Defense of Internment* is an instructive book in how this automatic assumption of racial discrimination may ignore reality. Although the internment of ethnic Japanese during World War II has often been cast as an act of sheer racism, Malkin presents an entirely different explanation. She argues that President Franklin D. Roosevelt's internment measures were based not on anti-Japanese racism but on a logical strategy of national defense, especially given the vulnerabilities of the United States to acts of internal sabotage. Malkin cites now-declassified information that shows that by mid-1941 the Japanese had set up an extensive espionage network along America's West Coast, recruiting Japanese Americans to conduct surveillance of military bases, shipyards, airfields, and ports. According to U.S. government estimates, thirty-five hundred ethnic Japanese in the United States were active supporters of the Japanese war effort.

There is perhaps no greater reform cause in U.S. history than the civil rights crusade. But over time, that crusade has lost its focus. It has gone from a moral crusade in which all society participated to a victimized ideology that has turned against the majority culture. Consequently, the fight against racial discrimination has morphed into a sometimes socially destructive force. It has imposed a culture of fear and silence instead of creating a more morally vibrant society. Moreover, this culture of fear and silence has become institutionalized in the nation's politics.

The assertion of racial discrimination charges has migrated far beyond the realm of combating specific racist attitudes and conduct. It has become incorporated into a much larger crusade of cultural liberalism. Given the guilt and defensiveness America feels over the issue of race, charges of racism are a powerful and indefensible weapon in weakening the shields of cultural values and institutions. And this weakening marks a necessary stage in the cultural revolution that began during the 1960s—a revolution that seeks to replace traditional cultural values with ones that are more secularist, socially divisive, antipatriotic, and anti-Western.

This attack on American values has not only eroded social bonds and diminished the public's allegiance to American civic institutions, it has also interfered with the very functioning of democratic government. Not surprisingly, given the Left's continual assault on traditional forms of social authority, contemporary polls show that only 22 percent of the public trusts the federal government.[1] Even aside from government, there has been a steady loss of confidence toward every kind of social institution. Since 1970, public confidence in universities, corporations, and the medical profession has dropped by more than half.[2] This mistrust and resulting adversity toward public institutions exemplified by a rather simple incident: the reaction of government employees to the Pentagon's recent decision to close its child-care center. Fearful that the Pentagon could be hit by another terrorist attack, officials decided to close the day-care center it operated for its employees' children. But this decision was met with outrage, even though Pentagon officials promised to build a new center in a safer location. Employees who used the day-care facility did not trust the government's stated motive, even though the Pentagon had suffered a deadly attack on September 11, 2001.[3]

Because race and racial politics have been recruited to the cause of cultural liberalism and its ideology of victimhood, racism claims must be scrutinized with this larger purpose in mind. Racism cannot be tolerated, but neither can the weakening of America's democratic and cultural foundations. An ideology of victimhood, fostered by a manipulated guilt over race, should not be allowed to distort governmental policies on such divergent issues as treatment of illegal aliens and the ability of the United States to assert its own foreign policy independent of the United Nations. Moreover, an ideology of victimhood, focusing almost exclusively on a combative individualism, undercuts any attempt to construct a unifying national ideology that can inspire diverse individuals to sacrifice some of their self-interests for those of the larger society.

The antidiscrimination crusade has spawned a fallout that has spread to every aspect of society, undermining centuries-old cultural values and institutions. The danger is that this fallout will continue to corrode cultural foundations until there is no identifying culture left, until society loses all unifying bonds, becoming simply a venue for various groups to air their grievances. The danger of such a culture of grievance is that, for all the grievances to be seen as legitimate, society as a whole must be seen as inherently oppressive, victimizing, and not worth saving.

Times change. This is a universal rule of life that applies even to the application of sacred principles such as civil rights and racial justice. What started out as a noble effort a half century ago has been diverted into an often socially divisive force. But no longer can the majority culture simply retreat from the racial debate. It cannot continue to shirk its responsibility in that area; nor can it allow its unconfronted guilt to direct the nation's social policies. Guilt is no path to truth, just as dwelling on one's victimhood is no path to justice.

NotEs

Chapter 1: IN THE WAKE OF THE ANTIDISCRIMINATION CRUSADE

1. "A Not-so-grand Homecoming," MSNBC.com, September 22, 2004.

2. Heather Knight, "School Accused of Racism," *San Francisco Chronicle*, June 28, 2004, http://sfgate.com/cgi-bin/article.cgi?f=/c/a/2004/06/28.

3. Eugene Volokh, "Is Criticizing Affirmative Action Illegal in Chicago?" Adversity.Net, September 1, 1999, www.adversity.net/special/freespeech.htm.

4. Arthur Coleman and Jonathan Alger, "Beyond Speech Codes," *Journal of College and University Law* 23 (1996): 91, 92.

5. Ibid., 115.

6. See Sara Rimer and Karen Arenson, "Top Colleges Take More Blacks, But Which Ones?" *New York Times*, June 24, 2004.

7. Anita Hamilton and Peter Bailey, "Recharging the Mission," *Time*, January 17, 2005, 50.

8. In 2005, minority homeownership exceeded 51 percent for the first time in history (Alphonso Jackson, "It Really Is Black and White," *Wall Street Journal*, April 19, 2005).

9. Larry Elder, "Democrats Again Play Race Card, But the Game May Soon End for Them," *Human Events*, January 13, 2005, www.humaneventsonline.com.

10. Mark Bauerlein, "Diversity Dropouts," *Weekly Standard*, September 27, 2004, 24.

11. Deborah Simmons, "Inferior Interior," *Washington Times*, August 20, 2004.

12. Kevin Diaz, "Kerry Decries Racial, Class Divide," *Minneapolis Star Tribune*, August 6, 2004.

13. Dinesh D'Souza, *The End of Racism: Principles for a Multiracial Society* (New York: Free Press, 1995), 320.

Chapter 2: THE FOG OF RACISM

1. Rhonda V. Magee Andrews, "Affirmative Action After Grutter: Reflections on a Tortured Death, Imagining a Humanity-Affirming Reincarnation," *Los Angeles Law Review* 63 (2003): 705, 714.

2. John H. McWhorter, "Still Losing the Race?" *Commentary*, February 2004, 37–38.

3. James Campbell, "Habits of Mind," *Dissent*, July 1, 2002, 92.

4. Kimberle Crenshaw, "Race, Reform and Retrenchment," *Harvard Law Review* 101 (1988): 1131.

5. Cornel West, *Keeping Faith: Philosophy and Race in America* (New York: Routledge, 1993), 236.

6. Derrick Bell, *Faces at the Bottom of the Well: The Permanence of Racism* (New York: Basic Books, 1992), 12.

7. Timothy Davis, "The Myth of the Superspade: The Persistence of Racism in College Athletics," *Fordham Urban Law Journal* 22 (Spring 1995): 615, 642.

8. Heather MacDonald, "The Black Cops You Never Hear About," *City Journal*, Summer 2002.

9. Nathan Glazer, *Affirmative Discrimination: Ethnic Inequality and Public Policy* (Cambridge, MA: Harvard University Press, 1987).

10. Dinesh D'Souza, *The End of Racism: Principles for a Multiracial Society* (New York: Free Press, 1995), 319.

11. Miriam Jordan, "Testing 'English Only' Rules," *Wall Street Journal*, November 18, 2005.

12. James Dao, "With Heady Days in the Past, Ex-Atlanta Mayor Faces Trial," *New York Times*, January 23, 2006.

13. Ibid.

14. Adam Nossiter, "Race Is at Fore as Vote Nears in New Orleans," *New York Times*, April 4, 2006.

15. Ibid.

16. Ibid.

17. Monica Davey, "Big Loser in a Polarizing, No-Holds-Barred Election Is Race Relations," *New York Times*, April 14, 2004.

18. T. Alexander Aleinikoff, "The Constitution in Context: The Continuing Significance of Racism," *Colorado Law Review* 63 (1992): 363.

19. See André Douglas Pond Cummings, "'Lions and Tigers and Bears, Oh My' or 'Redskins and Braves and Indians, Oh Why': Ruminations on McBride v. Utah State Tax Commission, Political Correctness and the Reasonable Person" *California Western Law Review* 36 (Fall 1999): 11.

20. Abby Goodnough, "Honor for Dr. King Splits Florida City, and Faces Reversal," *New York Times*, May 10, 2004.

21. Sari Horwitz, "Unlicensed College Provided D.C. Afrocentric Training," *Washington Post*, August 14, 1993; "Abena Walker's Curriculum," *Washington Times*, September 14, 1993; Sari Horwitz, "Participants Laud Afrocentric Program, Blast Media," *Washington Post*, September 23, 1994.

22. Jennifer Lee, "In New York's Most Diverse Police Class, Blue Comes in Many Colors," *New York Times*, July 8, 2005.

23. Andrew Murr, "Back on the Mean Streets," *Time*, February 21, 2005, 32.

24. Lena Williams, "Growing Black Debate: Racism or an Excuse?" *New York Times*, April 5, 1992.

25. Ibid.

26. Laurie Kellman, "Arrest Warrant Sought for Rep. McKinney," *Associated Press*, April 3, 2006, http://news.yahoo.com/s/ap/20060403.

27. Carl Hulse, "Congresswoman Accuses Capitol Police Officer of Racial Bias," *New York Times*, April 1, 2006.

28. Sheryl Gay Stolberg, "After Accusing Police of Racism, Congresswoman Apologizes," *New York Times*, April 7, 2006.

29. Joe R. Geagin and Melvin P. Likes, *Living with Racism* (Boston: Beacon Press, 1994), 20.

30. Martin Kilson and Clement Cottingham, "Thinking About Race Relations," *Dissent*, Fall 1991, 520–29.

31. Joel Kovel, *White Racism: A Psychohistory* (New York: Columbia University Press, 1984), xi, 32.

32. Molefi Kete Asante, *Afrocentricity* (Trenton, NJ: Africa World Press, 1988), 35.

33. Richard Majors and Jacob Gordon, eds., *The American Black Male* (Chicago: Nelson Hall, 1994), 171.

34. Ali A. Mazrui, "Dr. Schweitzer's Racism," *Transition* 53 (1991): 97.

35. Sut Jhally and Justin Lewis, *Enlightened Racism* (Boulder, CO: Westview Press, 1992).

36. Thomas Powell, "Feel Good Racism," *New York Times*, May 24, 1992.

37. Thomas West, "The Racist Other," http://jac.gsu.edu/jac/17.2/articles/5.htm.

38. William McGowan, *Coloring the News: How Crusading for Diversity Has Corrupted American Journalism* (San Francisco: Encounter Books, 2001), 46.

39. Amy Wax and Philip Telock, "We Are All Racists at Heart," *Wall Street Journal*, December 1, 2005.

40. Ibid.

41. D'Souza, *End of Racism*, 342.

42. Ibid., 348.

43. Bell, *Faces at the Bottom of the Well*, 5.

44. Johnetta Cole, *Conversations: Straight Talk with America's Sister President* (New York: Doubleday, 1993), 56.

45. Paul Farhi and Kevin Merida, "House Rejects Tax Break," *Washington Post*, February 22, 1995.

46. John Corry, "The Press's True Colors," *National Review*, December 31, 2001.

47. Anthony Lewis, "It Can Happen Here," *New York Times*, November 11, 1991.

48. Jennifer Hochschild, *The New American Dilemma* (New Haven: Yale University Press, 1984), 203.

49. David Brennen, "Race and Equality Across the Law School Curriculum: The Law of Tax Exemption," *Journal of Legal Education* 54 (September 2004): 336, 339.

50. Ibid., 354.

51. Associated Press, "Racial Profiling Rife in America," September 16, 2004, http://www.msnbc.msn.com/id/5988377/print/1/displaymode/1098/.

52. Deborah Simmons, "Sex and the American Schoolhouse," *Washington Times*, August 15, 2004.

53. Greg Allen, "The X Factor," *New York Times*, May 1, 2005 ("At next week's contemporary art auctions, work by women will go for a lot less than work by men. . . . Is the art market biased?").

54. "Uneasy Rests the Crown on 1997's Miss Colorado," *New York Times*, May 17, 1998.

55. Patrick M. Garry, *A Nation of Adversaries: How the Litigation Explosion Is Reshaping America* (New York: Plenum Press, 1997), 10.

56. Cullen Murphy, "Scapegoat," *Atlantic Monthly*, April 1995, 22.

57. Margaret Carlson, "And Now, Obesity Rights," *Time*, December 6, 1993, 96.

58. Richard Arum, "Sparing Rods, Spoiling Children," *National Review*, October 11, 2004, 44.

59. Associated Press, "Baltimore School Fight Arson Growth," *Augusta Chronicle*, November 13, 2004, 2004 WLNR 9857660

60. By the early 1990s, more than 60 percent of the nation's colleges and universities had adopted speech codes prohibiting racist speech; see Carolyn Mitchell, "The Political Correctness Doctrine: Redefining Speech on College Campuses," *Whittier Law Review* 13 (1992): 805, 818.

61. Victor Davis Hanson, "Topsy-Turvy," *National Review*, October 13, 2003, 38.

62. Ibid.

63. Dan Subotnik, *Toxic Diversity: Race, Gender and Law Talk in America* (New York: New York University Press, 2005).

64. See Kirk A. Kennedy, "Race-Exclusive Scholarships: Constitutional Vel Non," *Wake Forest Law Review* 30 (1995): 759, 795.

65. Ibid.

66. Ibid.

67. John McWhorter, "The Mau-Mauing at Harvard," *City Journal*, Spring 2002.

68. Garry, *A Nation of Adversaries*, 115.

69. "Even Columbus," *Wall Street Journal*, October 12, 1992.

70. Richard Delgado, "Campus Antiracism Rules," *Northwestern University Law Review* 85 (1991): 343, 351.

71. Ibid., 351.

72. Ibid., 353.

73. Brian Anderson, "Right on Campus," *Wall Street Journal*, January 14, 2005.

74. John Zmirak, "P.C.'s Second Wave," FrontPageMagazine.com, November 29, 2004.

75. Darryl Brown, "Racism and Race Relations in the University," *University of Virginia Law Review* 76 (1990): 295, 299.

76. See Thomas Ross, "Innocence and Affirmative Action," *Vanderbilt Law Review* 43 (1990): 297, 312 (describing blacks' being burdened by the persistence of unconscious racism); Charles Lawrence, "The Id, the Ego, and Equal Protection: Reckoning with Unconscious Racism," *Stanford Law Review* 39 (1987): 317, 321 (arguing that racism is an illness that "affects almost everyone").

77. T. Alexander Aleinikoff, "The Constitution in Context: The Continuing Significance of Racism," *University of Colorado Law Review* 63 (1992): 325, 352.

78. Ibid., 369–70.

79. McWhorter, "The Mau-Mauing at Harvard."

80. Lawrence, "The Id, the Ego, and Equal Protection," 317, 321.

81. Roger Kimball, "The Awful Truth," *City Journal*, Spring 2002.

82. McWhorter, "The Mau-Mauing at Harvard."

83. Brown, "Racism and Race Relations," 312, 322.

84. West, "The Racist Other."

85. Kent Kostka, "Higher Education, Hopwood, and Homogeneity: Preserving Affirmative Action and Diversity in a Scrutinizing Society," *Denver University Law Review* 74 (1996): 265, 279–80.

86. See Jed Rubenfeld, "Affirmative Action," *Yale Law Journal* 107 (1997): 427, 433.

87. Alex M. Johnson Jr., "The New Voice of Color," *Yale Law Journal* 100 (1991): 2007, 2052.

88. Brief of Amici Curiae NAACP Legal Defense and Educational Fund and the ACLU at 3, *Grutter v. Bollinger*, 123 S. Ct. 2325 (2003) (No. 02–241).

89. D'Souza, *End of Racism*, 489.

90. Ibid., 490.

91. Timothy Davis, "The Myth of the Superspade," *Fordham Urban Law Journal* 22 (1995): 615, 619.

92. Ibid., 659.

93. Ibid., 667.

94. Ibid., 674.

95. Ruth Intress, "Colleges in South Largely Segregated, Report Shows: Study Also Finds Subtle or Overt Racism," *Richmond Times-Dispatch*, May 18, 1995.

96. Robert Atwell, president of the American Council on Education, has characterized the legal arguments against racial preferences as "bogus"; see Elizabeth Shogren, "Minority-Based Scholarships OK," *Los Angeles Times*, February 18, 1994.

97. *Grutter* 123 S. Ct. 2325.

98. See Neal Devins, "Explaining Grutter v. Bollinger," *University of Pennsylvania Law Review* 152 (2003): 347, 368; see also Suzanne E. Eckes, "Race-Conscious Admissions Programs: Where Do Universities Go from Gratz and Grutter?" *Journal of Law and Education* 33 (2004): 21, 48.

99. See Eckes, "Race-Conscious Admissions Programs," 49, and Erwin Chemerinsky, "Making Sense of the Affirmative Action Debate," *Ohio Northern University Law Review* 22 (1996): 1159–60.

100. See Peter H. Schuck, "Affirmative Action: Past, Present, and Future," *Yale Law and Policy Review* (2002): 1, 9.

101. Chang-Lin Tien, "Diversity and Excellence in Higher Education," in *Debating Affirmative Action: Race, Gender, Ethnicity, and the Politics of Inclusion*, ed. Nicolaus Mills (New York: Delta, 1994), 237, 239

102. Benjamin F. Boyer et al., "Report of the Committee on Racial Discrimination," *1964 Association American Law Schools Proceedings*, pt. 1, 159–60.

103. Richard Sander, "A Systemic Analysis of Affirmative Action in American Law Schools," *Stanford Law Review* 57 (2004): 367, 378.

104. Ibid., 407–8, 410–11.

105. Ibid., 379.

106. Ibid., 386.

107. Ibid., 410.

108. David E. Bernstein, "Affirmative Blackmail," *Wall Street Journal*, February 11, 2006.

109. Schuck, "Affirmative Action," 36; see also Rachel Zabarkes Friedman, "Waking Up," *National Review*, October 13, 2003, 44 (describing student dissatisfaction with "the radical left-wing views of their professors").

110. David Brooks, "People Like Us," *Atlantic Monthly*, September 2003, 32 (noting that of the forty-two professors in the English, history, sociology, and political science departments at Brown University, all were Democrats).

111. John Tierney, "Republicans Outnumbered in Academia, Studies Find," *New York Times*, November 18, 2004.

112. "Faculty Members Do Lean to the Left, Study Shows," *Sioux Falls Argus Leader*, March 30, 2005.

113. Karl Zinsmeister, "Diversity on Campus? There Is None," *American Enterprise Online*, January 7, 2005.

114. Ibid.; see also Jeff Jacoby, "Intellectual Diversity? Not on Campus," Townhall.com, December 4, 2004, www.townhall.com/columnists/jeffjacoby/printjj20041204.html.

115. Yilu Zhao, "Taking the Liberalism Out of Liberal Arts," *New York Times*, April 3, 2004.

116. According to data compiled by the nonpartisan Center for Responsive Politics.

117. Ruth R. Wisse, "John Kerry U," *Wall Street Journal*, October 25, 2004.

118. See *Martin v. Wilks*, 490 U.S. 755 (1989); *United States v. Paradise*, 480 U.S. 149 (1987); *Local No. 93, Int'l .Ass'n. of Firefighters v. Cleveland*, 478 U.S. 501 (1986); *Firefighters Local Union No. 1784 v. Stotts*, 467 U.S. 561 (1984).

119. *Church of the Holy Trinity v. United States*, 143 U.S. 457, 463 (1892).

120. Patrick Healy and Sara Rimer, "Furor Lingers as Harvard Chief Gives Details of Talk on Women," *New York Times*, February 18, 2005.

121. Amanda Ripley, "Who Says a Woman Can't Be Einstein?" *Time*, March 7, 2005, 51.

122. Victor Davis Hanson, "Teachable Moments," *National Review*, March 14, 2005, 17.

123. Christina Hoff Sommers, "Summers Storm," *National Review*, February 14, 2005, 26.

124. Linda Chavez, "Mathematical Virtues," *Washington Times*, January 22, 2005.

125. Ripley, "Who Says a Woman Can't Be Einstein?" 52; Walter E. Williams, "Anti-Intellectualism at Harvard," *Washington Times*, March 19, 2005.

126. Chavez, "Mathematical Virtues"; Jacob Sullum, "The Brain Storm," *Washington Times*, January 24, 2005.

127. Charles Murray, "The Inequality Taboo," *Commentary*, September 2005, 13.

128. Ibid., 22.

129. Eric Adler and Jack Langer, "The Intifada Comes to Duke," *Opinion Journal*, January 5, 2005, www.opinionjournal.com.

130. Ibid.

131. Ibid.

Chapter 3: AWASH IN CONTRADICTIONS

1. Stephen Kinzer, "Debating a Plan for a Blacks-Only Fund to Finance an 'Africa Town' in Detroit," *New York Times*, October 13, 2004.

2. Editorial, "Mad in Motown," *Wall Street Journal*, October 1, 2004.

3. Sarah Karush, "Detroit African Town Plan Stirs Debate," October 10, 2004, http://news.yahoo.com/news?tmpl=story&cid=519&u=/ap/20041010/ap_on_re_us/detroit.

4. Amicus brief in *Grutter v. Bollinger* of the Society of American Law Teachers, 2003 WL 399060, 1.

5. Erica Frankenberg, Chungmei Lee, and Gary Orfield, *A Multiracial Society with Segregated Schools: Are We Losing the Dream?* (Cambridge, MA: Civil Rights Project, Harvard University, 2003), 50. Many civil rights activists claim that the white exodus from Detroit is demographic testimony to racism, but this "white flight" did not take place when blacks began migrating to Detroit in the early twentieth century; it did not significantly occur until after the violent and widespread inner-city riots of the late 1960s.

6. K. Bradsher, "Nouvelle Detroit? Global Growth Brings Changes at Home," *New York Times*, October 16, 1997.

7. Native American Recognition Bill, S. 344 and HR 665, 108th Congress (2004).

8. Gary Orfield, Susan E. Eaton, and the Harvard Project on School Desegregation, *Dismantling Desegregation: The Quiet Reversal of Brown v. Board of Education* (New York: New Press, 1996).

9. Reginald Oh, "Re-Mapping Equal Protection Jurisprudence," *American University Law Review* 53 (2005): 1305, 1310.

10. Rachel L. Swarns, "Hispanics Resist Racial Grouping by Census," *New York Times*, October 24, 2004.

11. Ramesh Ponnuru, "Affirmative Reaction," www.uiowa.edu/~030116/116/articles/ponnuru.htm.

12. Ibid.

13. Ibid.

14. Walter Williams, "Gleaned from the Fine Print," *Washington Times*, July 3, 1992.

15. Stephan Thernstrom and Abigail Thernstrom, "Reflections on *The Shape of the River*," *UCLA Law Review* 46 (1999): 1583, 1607.

16. Heather MacDonald, "Heralds of a Brighter Black Future," *City Journal*, Spring 2005, www.city-journal.org/html/15_2_heralds.html.

17. Heather MacDonald, "Reporting While Wrong," *National Review*, September 26, 2005, 43.

18. Heather MacDonald, "The Black Cops You Never Hear About," *City Journal*, Summer 2002, www.city-journal.org/html/12_3_black_cops.html.

19. Scott Johnson, "Better Safe and (Occasionally) Sorry," *American Enterprise*, January–February 2003, www.taemag.com/issues/articleID.1735/article_detail.asp

20. Ibid.; Heather MacDonald, "The Racial Profiling Myth Debunked," *City Journal*, Spring 2002, www.city-journal.org/html/12_2_the_racial_profiling.html.

21. Heather MacDonald, "Don't Poison Policing with Racial Politics," *Hartford Courant*, October 10, 2004, www.manhattan-institute.org/html/_hartfordc_dont_poison.html.

22. Ibid.

23. William McGowan, *Coloring the News: How Crusading for Diversity Has Corrupted American Journalism* (San Francisco: Encounter Books, 2001), 75.

24. Dinesh D'Souza, *The End of Racism: Principles for a Multiracial Society* (New York: Free Press, 1995), 283.

25. Andrew Hacker, *Two Nations: Black and White, Separate, Hostile, Unequal* (New York: Scribner, 2003), 197.

26. Cited by Lynne Duke, "Confronting Violence," *Washington Post*, January 8, 1994.

27. Johnetta Cole, *Conversations: Straight Talk with America's Sister President* (New York: Doubleday, 1993), 46.

28. Christine Kearney, "Activists Hold Hip-Hop Political Convention," *Reuters*, June 19, 2004.

29. Damien Cave, "In a Divided Town, a Question of Hate, or Cash?" *New York Times*, October 24, 2004.

30. Miriam Jordan, "Blacks vs. Latinos at Work," *Wall Street Journal*, January 24, 2006.

31. Anderson Thompson, "The Los Angeles Rebellion: Seizing the Historical Moment," in *Why L.A. Happened: Implications of the '92 Los Angeles Rebellion*, ed. Haki R. Madhubuti (Chicago: Third World Press, 1993), 49–59.

32. Ice Cube, *Death Certificate*, Priority Records, 1991.

33. National Conference on Christians and Jews, Taking America's Pulse: The National Conference Survey on Intergroup Relations, 6–11.

34. McGowan, *Coloring the News*, 60 (citing surveys showing that blacks are at least three times more likely to commit hate crimes against whites than vice versa).

35. Anti-Defamation League, "ADL Survey on Anti-Semitism and Prejudice in America," November 16, 1992, 30–32; Jennifer Golub, "What Do We Know About Black Anti-Semitism?" American Jewish Committee Working Paper, New York, 1990, 21, 28–29; Harold Quinley and Charles Y. Glock, *Anti-Semitism in America* (New Brunswick, NJ: Transaction Books, 1983), xx, 55, 70.

36. Danyel Smith, "Harry Allen: Hip Hop's Intellectual Assassin," *San Francisco Weekly*, February 13, 1991.

37. Sean Piccoli, "Malcolm X, the Legacy: Does Black Racism Exist?" *Washington Times*, November 18, 1992.

38. Whitney Young, *Beyond Racism* (New York: McGraw-Hill, 1969), 85.

39. George Garriguez, "National Merit Scholarships: A Major Dash of Jim Crow," *Journal of Blacks in Higher Education* 3 (Spring 1994): 60–64.

40. Dana Boone, "Report: Blacks Suspended at High Rate," DesMoinesRegister .com, August 3, 2004.

41. Ibid.

42. Joel Schwartz, "Explaining Black Underachievement," *Public Interest* (Summer 2003): 152.

43. Signithia Fordham and John Ogbu, "Black Student School Success: Coping with the Burden of Acting White," *Urban Review* 18, no. 3 (1986), 176–206.

44. Marc Elrich, "The Stereotype Within," *Educational Leadership*, April 1994, 13.

45. Ellis Cose, "Does Cosby Help?" *Newsweek*, December 27, 2004, 66.

46. John McWhorter, "The Campus Diversity Fraud," *City Journal*, Winter 2002, www.city-journal.org/html/12_1_the_campus.html.

47. James Taranto, "What's Behind Liberal Racism," WSJ.com Opinion Journal, December 10, 2004.

48. Jewelle Taylor Gibbs, ed., *Young, Black and Male in America: An Endangered Species* (Dover, MA: Auburn House, 1988), 19.

49. Thomas Sowell, "Crippled by Their Culture," *Wall Street Journal*, April 26, 2005.

50. Ibid.

51. Piccoli, "Malcolm X."

52. D'Souza, *End of Racism*, 485.

53. Orlando Patterson, "A Poverty of the Mind," *New York Times*, March 26, 2006.

54. Ibid.

55. Heather MacDonald, "The Immigrant Gang Plague," *City Journal*, Summer 2004.

56. These statistics are reported in John F. McDonald, "The Decline of Social and Economic Problems in America," *Milken Institute Review* (Second Quarter 2004): 46.

57. Oh, "Re-Mapping Equal Protection Jurisprudence," 1305, 1344. However,

in yet another contradiction, the economic status of blacks living within jurisdictions governed by African American political leaders has declined (ibid.).

58. Michelle Malkin, "Jacko and Snoop Dogg's America," *Washington Times*, February 5, 2005.

59. Adam Liptak, "U.S. Suits Multiply, But Fewer Ever Get to Trial, Study Says," *New York Times*, December 14, 2003.

60. Susan Mandel, "Empirical Study Suggests Bias in U.S. Appellate Courts," December 26, 2003, http://www.findjustice.com/ms/news/review.php?id=22&id1=8.

61. Ibid.

62. Paul Craig Roberts and Lawrence M. Stratton, *The New Color Line: How Quotas and Privilege Destroy Democracy* (Washington, DC: Regnery, 1995), 89.

63. "The Challenge of Managing Diversity in the Workplace," *Black Enterprise*, July 1993, 90; Drew Clark, "Getting Along: Workplace Diversity Consultants Take Corporate World by Storm," *Washington Business Journal*, March 25–31, 1994, 29, 32.

64. Erik Eckholm, "Plight Deepens for Black Men, Studies Warn," *New York Times*, March 20, 2006.

65. Ibid.

66. With respect to disciplinary actions, the evidence shows that black and Hispanic officers were indeed punished more frequently than whites, but only for offenses that carry mandatory discipline, such as drug use or criminal behavior. The NYPD disciplinary records reveal that black male officers failed drug tests four times as often as white male officers, and received mandatory discipline for off-duty offenses like assault and grand larceny nearly three times as often as whites. MacDonald, "The Black Cops You Never Hear About."

67. Larry Elder, "60 Minutes Blows It on Black/White Adoption," *Human Events Online*, February 24, 2005.

68. "Study Finds Blacks Miss Prostrate Cancer Tests," http://www.msnbc.msn.com/id/6115510/print/1/displaymode/1098?

69. "Minority Children Get Less Sleep, Study Finds," http"//www.msnbc.msn.com/id/6173884/print/1/displaymode/1098/.

70. McGowan, *Coloring the News*, 204.

71. Ibid., 210.

72. Ibid., 68.

73. Ibid., 60.

74. Ibid., 221.

75. Ibid., 192.

76. Statement by Gregory Favre, *Sacramento Bee*, November 2, 1991.

77. Robert Lichter, Linda Lichter, and Stanley Rothman, *Watching America* (New York: Prentice Hall, 1991), 198.

78. "Imagine That," *Washington Times*, April 1, 1992.

79. A sampling of movie critic headlines make the point: Alessandra Stanley, "Old-Time Sexism Suffuses New Season," *New York Times*, October 1, 2004; Motoko Rich, "The Season's Japan Movies: Naive, Racist, Well-Intended, Accurate—or All of the Above?" *New York Times*, January 4, 2004.

80. Sut Jhally and Justin Lewis, *Enlightened Racism: The Cosby Show, Audiences and the Myth of the American Dream* (Bolder, CO: Westview Press, 1992), 74, 91, 97, 110.

Chapter 4: THE ONLY SIN IN A CULTURE OF MORAL RELATIVISM

1. David Frum, *How We Got Here: The Decade That Brought You Modern Life* (New York: Basic Books, 2000).

2. James Lincoln Collier, *The Rise of Selfishness in America* (New York: Oxford University Press, 1994).

3. James Q. Wilson, *The Moral Sense* (New York: Simon and Schuster, 1993), 61.

4. Gertrude Himmelfarb, *The De-Moralization of Society: From Victorian Virtues to Modern Virtues* (New York: Knopf, 1995).

5. One of the linguistic legacies of the Bill Clinton presidency was the "move-on" mantra. Almost as soon as it was revealed that the president had committed a felony by lying under oath, that he may have tried to obstruct a federal criminal investigation, and that he may have sexually accosted a female volunteer in the Oval Office, his supporters began an endless repetition of the plea that the country just move on. When the Clinton-Gore fund-raising scandals arose, the move-on

mantra was revived, just as it was when long-subpoenaed documents were mysteriously discovered in the Clinton residential quarters of the White House.

6. Michael Corin, "Quantifying America's Decline," *Wall Street Journal*, March 15, 1993.

7. During a riot that ensued after the University of Connecticut won the men's NCAA basketball tournament in 2004, students and fans overturned cars and set several fires. "It was just completely out of control," an observer said. "They burned anything they could find" (Laura Walsh, "UConn Takes Action Against Rowdy NCAA Celebrators," Newsday.com, April 9, 2004).

8. Barbara Dafoe Whitehead, "The Failure of Sex Education," *Atlantic Monthly*, October 1994, 55–80.

9. Victor Davis Hanson, "Topsy-Turvy," *National Review*, October 13, 2003, 36.

10. Ibid.

11. William McGowan, *Coloring the News: How Crusading for Diversity Has Corrupted American Journalism* (San Francisco: Encounter Books, 2001), 58.

12. Stefan Beck, "Survival of Culture," *Dartmouth Review*, March 23, 2003, www.dartreview.com/archives/2003/03/23/survival_.

13. Michelle Malkin, "Grace, Gratitude and God," *Washington Times*, November 25, 2004.

14. John McWhorter, "The Campus Diversity Fraud," *City Journal*, Winter 2002, www.city-journal.org/html/12_1_the_campus.html; Michael Greve, "The Newest Move in Law Schools' Quota Game," *Wall Street Journal*, October 5, 1992.

15. Nick Madigan, "Los Angeles Moves to Ease Tensions After Tape Captures Police Beating of Black Suspect," *New York Times*, June 25, 2004.

16. Heather MacDonald, "Heralds of a Brighter Black Future," *City Journal*, Spring 2005, www.city-journal.org/html/15_2_heralds.html.

17. Jill Steward, "Rasta Republican," *Wall Street Journal*, April 28, 2005.

18. Karen Arenson, "Duke Grappling with Impact of Scandal on Its Reputation," *New York Times*, April 7, 2006.

19. The study was conducted by Penn and Shoen Associates, Inc., in March 1994 and was reported in the April 1994 issue of *National Law Journal*.

20. Andrew Tilghman, "Baytown Man Given a 10-Year Sentence," *Houston*

Chronicle, September 22, 2004; "Woman to Seek Testing for Staging Crime," *American Renaissance News*, September 18, 2004.

21. Joshua Kaplowitz, "How I Joined Teach for America—and Got Sued for $20 Million," *City Journal*, Winter 2003, www.city-journal.org/html/13_1_how_i_joined.html.

22. McGowan, *Coloring the News*, 20.

23. Dave Harris, *Quincy Patriot Ledger*, 2004.

24. Jeremy Meyer, "Workers Fighting English-Only Rules," *Denver Post*, November 18, 2004.

25. Heather MacDonald, "Time to Take Illegal Immigration Seriously," *City Journal*, September 2004, www.city-journal.org/html/eon_09_16_04hm.html.

26. Jeffrey Mazzella, "Real ID Vital to Security," *Washington Times*, February 20, 2005.

27. Graham Schmidt, "Civil Rights Voting Case Under Investigation: Prairie View A&M Students Say Their Rights Were Violated," *Daily Texan*, February 10, 2004.

28. Heather MacDonald, "Straighten Up and Fly Right," *Wall Street Journal*, December 2, 2004.

29. Charisse Jones, "Many Scoff at N.J. Ruling Over Ladies Nights," *USA Today*, June 4, 2004.

30. Michael Hierstand, "Announcer Apologizes for Poor Analogy to Rodney King Incident," *USA Today*, October 21, 2004.

31. Shelby Steele, "White Guilt = Black Power," *Wall Street Journal*, January 8, 2002.

32. Ibid.

33. Harry Stein, "How I Was Smeared," *City Journal*, Autumn 2002, www.city-journal.org/html/12_4_how_i_was.html.

34. McGowan, *Coloring the News*, 236.

35. See Shelby Steele, *The Content of Our Character: A New Vision of Race in America* (New York: HarperPerennial, 1991), 79–80.

36. Ibid., 87–88.

37. Shelby Steele, "Live with TAE," *American Enterprise*, April 2006, 16.

38. James Q. Wilson, "American Dilemma," *National Review*, December 19, 2005, 61.

39. MacDonald, "Heralds of a Brighter Black Future."

40. Bernard Goldberg, *Arrogance: Rescuing America from the Media Elite* (New York: Warner Books, 2003), quoted in Frank Borzellieri, "Arrogantly Biased," American Renaissance, October 2004, www.amren.com/0410issue/0410issue.html.

41. MacDonald, "Heralds of a Brighter Black Future."

42. Heather MacDonald, "Reporting While Wrong," *National Review*, September 26, 2005, 44.

Chapter 5: A MORAL EROSION

1. Ross Douthat, "The Truth About Harvard," *Atlantic Monthly*, March 2005, 96.

2. Christopher Lasch, *The Revolt of the Elites and the Betrayal of Democracy* (New York: Norton, 1995), 84–85.

3. Michael Slackman, "Sharpton Shrugs Off Issues About His Tangled Finances," *New York Times*, January 10, 2004.

4. Ibid.

5. "R. Kelly Gig at Conference Draws Concerns," ABCNews.com, September 16, 2004, http://abclocal.go.com/wls/story?section=News&id=2125737.

6. Heather MacDonald, "Heralds of a Brighter Black Future," *City Journal*, Spring 2005, www.city-journal.org/html/15_2_heralds.html.

7. John McWhorter, "Why Blacks Don't Need Leaders," *City Journal*, Summer 2002, www.city-journal.org/html/12_3_why_blacks.html.

8. Robert Hampton, *Violence in the Black Family* (Lexington, MA: Lexington Books, 1987), x.

9. Dinesh D'Souza, *The End of Racism: Principles for a Multiracial Society* (New York: Free Press, 1995), 515.

10. Felicia R. Lee, "Cosby Defends His Remarks About Poor Blacks' Values," *New York Times*, May 22, 2004.

11. Jack Greenberg, "Diversity, the University, and the World Outside," *Columbia Law Review* 103 (2003): 1610.

12. John McWhorter, "Seduced: How Radical Ideas on Welfare, Work and Family Sent Poor Black Americans to Hell," *American Enterprise*, April 2006, 33.

13. Ibid., 34.

14. Dan Subotnik, *Toxic Diversity: Race, Gender and Law Talk in America* (New York: New York University Press, 2005), quoted in John O. McGinnis, "At Law School, Unstrict Scrutiny," Wall Street Journal, July 30, 2005, www.opinionjournal. com/?id=110007027.

15. Carter, *Civility*, 67.

16. McWhorter, "Seduced," 30.

17. Ibid., 32.

18. "Contrary Mary Frances Berry," *Washington Times*, December 8, 2004. Previously, Berry had refused to seat one of President Bush's appointees to the commission until a court ordered her to do so. See Mona Charen, "Civil Rights Led Amiss," WashingtonTimes.com, December 14, 2004.

19. Larry Elder, "Children Having Children," *Washington Times*, December 28, 2004.

20. See, e.g., Stephanie Coontz, *The Way We Never Were: American Families and the Nostalgia Trap* (New York: Basic Books, 1992), for a summary of the views of family life that became common in the 1960s and 1970s.

21. Daniel Patrick Moynihan, *The Negro Family: The Case for National Action*, U.S. Departmentof Labor, Office of Planning and Research, Washington, DC, 1965.

22. Daniel Patrick Moynihan, *Family and Nation* (San Diego: Harcourt, Brace, Jovanovich, 1986), 9.

23. Heather MacDonald, "The Immigrant Gang Plague," *City Journal*, Summer 2004, www.city-journal.org/html/14_3_immigrant_gang.html.

24. Ellis Cose, "Long After the Alarm Went Off," *Newsweek*, March 14, 2005, 37.

25. Ibid.

26. Steven Ruggles, "The Origins of African-American Family Structure," *American Sociological Review* 59, no. 1 (1994): 140.

27. Charles Krauthammer, "Defining Deviancy Up," *New Republic*, November 22, 1993, 20–25.

28. Gertrude Himmelfarb, *The De-Moralization of Society: From Victorian Virtues to Modern Virtues* (New York: Knopf, 1995).

29. D'Souza, *The End of Racism*, 511.

30. Lev Grossman, "I Am Still Tom Wolfe," *Time*, November 8, 2004, 74–75.

31. Walter E. Williams, "Tolerating School Violence," *Washington Times*, October 16, 2004.

32. Michelle Malkin, "Bordering on Enforcement," *Washington Times*, December 4, 2004.

33. William A. Galston, "Liberal Virtues and the Formation of Civic Character," in *Seedbeds of Virtue: Sources of Competence, Character, and Citizenship in American Society*, ed. Mary Ann Glendon and David Blankenhorn (New York: Madison Books, 1995), 43.

34. Heather MacDonald, "The Black Cops You Never Hear About," *City Journal*, Summer 2002, www.city-journal.org/html/12_3_black_cops.html.

35. Tony Kennedy, "A United Front Against Racism: Black Religious Leaders Praise Flynn for Speaking Out," *Minneapolis Star Tribune*, December 3, 2003.

36. Archbishop Harry J. Flynn, "In God's Image: Pastoral Letter on Racism," 6.

37. Ibid., 13.

38. Ibid., 19.

39. John McWhorter, "Who Should Get into College?" *City Journal*, Spring 2003, www.city-journal.org/html/13_2_who_should_get.html.

40. Federalist No. 55 (Madison).

41. Galston, "Liberal Virtues and the Formation of Civic Character," 38, 39.

42. J. Brian Benestad, "Ordinary Virtue as Heroism," in *Seedbeds of Virtue: Sources of Competence, Character, and Citizenship in American Society*, ed. Mary Ann Glendon and David Blankenhorn (New York: Madison Books, 1995), 238.

43. Robert Wuthnow, *Acts of Compassion: Caring for Others and Helping Ourselves* (Princeton, NJ: Princeton University Press, 1991), 115.

Chapter 6: THE POLITICAL PERPETUATION OF RACISM

1. See, e.g., Diana Jean Schemo, "Federal Program on Vouchers Draws Strong Minority Support," *New York Times*, April 6, 2006.

2. Ellis Cose, "A Dream Deferred," *Newsweek*, May 17, 2004, 59.

3. Jonathan Zimmerman, "Culture Wars Won't Win Black Vote for Bush," *Minneapolis Star Tribune*, August 3, 2004.

4. Stephen L. Carter, *The Culture of Disbelief: How American Law and Politics Trivialize Religious Devotion* (New York: Basic Books, 1993), 60.

5. Zell Miller, "Telling It Like It Is," *Wall Street Journal*, September 13, 2004.

6. Jonah Goldberg, "Raining Race," *National Review*, September 26, 2005, 12.

7. Theodore Dalrymple, "The Veneer of Civilization," *National Review*, September 26, 2005, 24.

8. David Horowitz, "It's Time for Fairness and Inclusion in Our Universities," FrontPageMagazine.com, December 14, 2004, www.frontpagemag.com/articles /printable.as;?ID=16301.

9. "Celebrities Uncensored," *Wall Street Journal*, July 30, 2004, 2004 WLNR 3364499.

10. "Bush to Speak to National Urban League," July 15, 2004, http://story.news .yahoo.com/news?tmpl=story&cid=536&e=6&u=/ap/2004071.

11. "Civil Rights and Wrongs," *Wall Street Journal*, July 19, 1990, 1990 WLNR 1460613.

12. Michael Sokolove, "Why Is Michael Steele a Republican Candidate?" *New York Times Magazine*, March 26, 2006, 36.

13. John McManus, "CBC: Dissension in the Ranks," *New American*, September 6, 1993, 17; Frank McCoy, "Can the Black Caucus Be Bipartisan?" *Black Enterprise*, January 1994, 22.

14. Edward Kennedy, quoted in Art Moore, "Democrats Accused of Racism," *WorldNetDaily*, November 19, 2003.

15. Editorial, "Sen. Reid's Remarks," *Washington Times*, December 9, 2004.

16. Moreover, it was former Ku Klux Klansman Sen. Robert Byrd (D-WV) who held up Rice's confirmation. "The Dems' Klan Card," Newsmax.com, January 21, 2005, www.frontpage.com/articles/printable.asp?ID=16718.

17. "Women's Group Denounces Racist Cartoons," United Press International, November 19, 2004.

18. "Black Clergy Denounces Racial Motivated Attacks," Townhall.com, November 21, 2004.

19. The Reverend Jesse Lee Peterson, quoted in James Taranto, "Liberal Racism," WSJ.com, November 18, 2004.

20. Randal C. Archibold, "Connecticut Senator Regrets His 'Poor Choice of Words,'" *New York Times*, April 16, 2004.

21. Howard Dean, quoted in Deborah Simmons, "Lye Soap and Racist Jokes," *Washington Times*, February 18, 2005.

22. David Kirkpatrick, "Bush Appeal to Churches Seeking Help Raises Doubts," *New York Times*, July 2, 2004.

23. John M. Glionna, "Nov. 2 is V-Day for Blacks in Florida," *Los Angeles Times*, October 11, 2004. The Democratic National Committee even asked black pastors to distribute campaign materials; see David Kirkpatrick, "Kerry Is Criticized for Church Drive," *New York Times*, October 13, 2004.

24. William A. Donohue, *Twilight of Liberty: The Legacy of the ACLU* (New Brunswick, NJ: Transaction, 1994), 120.

25. Shelby Steele, "Live with TAE," *American Enterprise*, April 2006, 13.

26. Jo Becker, "Black Leaders Protest Difficulties in Florida Vote Registration," *Boston Globe*, October 17, 2004.

27. Representative Jesse Jackson Jr., quoted in Jennifer Braceras, "Fearful Voters?" *Washington Times*, October 17, 2004.

28. A county commissioner of Gadsden County noted that 88 percent of county voters completed their ballots correctly. "If you're a teacher and 9 out of 10 students pass the test, I don't think the 12% should start complaining," he said (Glionna, "Nov. 2 Is V-Day for Blacks in Florida").

29. Andrew Welsh-Huggins, "Criticisms Mount Over Ohio Election Chief," Associated Press, October 6, 2004.

30. Robert McFadden, "Long Lines, Short Tempers, Little Chaos at Polls," *New York Times*, November 3, 2004. In the battleground state of Ohio, none of the hundreds of election lawyers and observers reported any major problems (Mark Landsbaum, "Kerry's Disenfranchisement Demagoguery," FrontPageMagazine.com, January 21, 2005). Nonetheless, two months after the election, Kerry alleged that "thousands of people were suppressed in their efforts to vote" (ibid.).

31. Jonah Goldberg, "The Myth of the Disenfranchised," *Washington Times*, October 22, 2004.

32. Abby Goodnough, "In '04 Florida, Lawsuits Begin Before Election," *New York Times*, October 14, 2004.

33. "Ohio Provisional Ballot Ruling Reversed," *Yahoo News*, October 23, 2004.

34. Thomas Crampton, "Worldwide Scrutiny of the U.S. Election Is Coming," *New York Times*, October 10, 2004.

35. In *Stealing Elections: How Voter Fraud Threatens Our Democracy*, author John Fund discloses that at least eight of the nineteen 9/11 hijackers were eligible to vote.

36. Mona Charen, "Uninvited to the Polls," *Washington Times*, October 26, 2004.

37. Michael Kelly, "Playing with Fire," *New Yorker*, July 15, 1996, 29.

38. Ibid., 31.

39. Ibid., 32.

40. Al Gore, quoted in Michael Fumento, "Who's Fanning the Flames of Racism?" *Wall Street Journal*, June 16, 1997.

41. In *Unholy Alliance: Radical Islam and the American Left* (Washington, DC: Regnery, 2004), David Horowitz shows that what unites the American Left and Islamism is a deep-seated hatred of the United States.

42. Duncan Currie, "Another War He Didn't Like," *Weekly Standard*, September 27, 2004, 16.

43. Senator Evan Bayh, quoted in David Greising, "The New Face of Money in U.S. Politics: Soros Is Spending Big to Oust Bush," *Chicago Tribune*, July 25, 2004.

44. R. Emmett Tyrrell, "A Republican for Dinner?" *Washington Times*, November 12, 2004.

Chapter 7: IN THE WAKE OF RACE

1. Barbara Johnson, ed., *Freedom and Interpretation: The Oxford Amnesty Lectures* (New York: Basic Books, 1993), 7.

2. Toni Morrison, "Unspeakable Things Unspoken: The Afro-American Presence in American Literature," *Michigan Quarterly Review* (Winter 1989): 8. Stokely Carmichael wanted to lead "a movement that will smash everything Western civilization has created." C. Vann Woodward, *The Strange Career of Jim Crow* (New York: Oxford University Press, 1974), 197–98.

3. Ishmael Reed, *Airing Dirty Laundry* (Reading, MA: Addison-Wesley, 1993), 87.

4. After a protest condemning a required course in Western civilization at Stanford University as teaching racism, the university dropped the course. Robert H. Bork, *Slouching Towards Gomorrah: Modern Liberalism and American Decline* (New York: Regan, 1996), 247.

5. A Pew Hispanic Center poll taken eight months after the patriotic high point of 9/11 proves Huntington's point. The poll revealed that among American citizens of Mexican descent, 55 percent considered themselves Mexican "first," 25 percent considered themselves primarily Latinos or Hispanics, and only 18 percent considered themselves Americans "first."

6. Alston B. Ramsay, "Hawaii Five-No," *National Review*, September 26, 2005, 35.

7. *South Bend Tribune*, July 23, 2004.

8. Elijah Anderson, "The Code of the Streets," *Atlantic Monthly*, May 1994, 83.

9. Ibid., 94.

10. Pete Hamill, "End Game," *Esquire*, December 1994, 86.

11. William Rhoden, "No Innocents in NBA Brawl at Game in Suburban Detroit," *New York Times*, November 21, 2004.

12. Kent Youngblood, "Timberwolf Arrested in Indianapolis," *Minneapolis Star Tribune*, November 26, 2004.

13. What is also remarkable is that when some of the nation's biggest sports stars admitted to using banned steroids in December 2004, the public was barely surprised. Mark Starr, "High," *Newsweek*, December 13, 2004, 32.

14. Edward Wong, "New Rules for Soccer Parents," *New York Times*, May 6, 2001.

15. Ibid.

16. "Resegregation's Aftermath," *Atlantic Monthly*, July–August 2004, 64. Unruly behavior, however, is not confined to the youth. The Reverend Fred Shuttlesworth was chosen president of the Southern Christian Leadership Conference by a convention in which order had to be restored by police. Clarence Page, "From Civil Rights to Cosby Values," *Washington Times*, December 3, 2004.

17. Sara Rimer, "Unruly Students Facing Arrest, Not Detention," *New York Times*, January 4, 2004.

18. Charles Murray, "The Hallmark of the Underclass," *Wall Street Journal*, September 29, 2005.

19. Ibid.

20. Erik Eckholm, "Plight Deepens for Black Men, Studies Warn," *New York Times*, March 20, 2006.

21. Ibid.

22. Ibid.

23. Mary Eberstadt, *Home-Alone America: The Hidden Toll of Day Care, Behavioral Drugs, and Other Parent Substitutes* (New York: Sentinel, 2004).

24. Zena Smith Blau, *Black Children, White Children: Competence, Socialization and Social Structure* (New York: Free Press, 1981), xv, 58.

25. Robert Rector, "How Not to Be Poor," *National Review*, October 24, 2005, 26.

26. Bell Hooks, *Yearning: Race, Gender and Cultural Politics* (Boston: South End Press, 1990), 76.

27. Alice Walker, "Not for Her," *Insight*, September 13, 1992, 18.

28. *The American Enterprise*, October–November 2004, 45.

29. Dinesh D'Souza, *The End of Racism: Principles for a Multiracial Society* (New York: Free Press, 1995), 499.

30. Cedric Jennings, quoted in Ron Susskind, "In Rough City School, Top Students Struggle to Learn," *Wall Street Journal*, May 26, 1994.

31. Roger Kimball, "Institutionalizing Our Demise: America vs. Multiculturalism," *New Criterion*, June 2004.

32. Ibid.

33. Fareed Zakaria, "Rejecting the Next Bill Gates," *Newsweek*, November 29, 2004, 33. Since the mid-1990s, the United States has been losing its worldwide dominance in the sciences, as indicated by a decline in the number of prizes awarded to American scientists, the number of published scientific papers, the number of patents for scientific inventions, and the number of graduate students in sciences. William Broad, "U.S. Is Losing Its Dominance in the Sciences," *New York Times*, May 3, 2004.

34. "Race Norming," *Wall Street Journal*, April 4, 1991.

35. Richard Seymour, "Why Plaintiffs' Counsel Challenge Tests, and How They Can Successfully Challenge the Theory of Validity Generalization," *Journal of Vocational Behavior* 33 (1988): 331–64.

36. "The Thin White Line," *U.S. News & World Report*, August 15, 1994, 53–54.

37. D'Souza, *End of Racism*, 459

38. Richard J. Herrnstein and Charles Murray, *The Bell Curve: Intelligence and Class Structure in American Life* (New York: Simon & Schuster, 1996), 282; Arthur Jensen, *Bias in Mental Testing* (New York: Basic Books, 1980), 552.

39. James Crouse and Dale Trusheim, *The Case Against the SAT* (Chicago: University of Chicago Press, 1988), 96–98.

40. D'Souza, *End of Racism*, 292.

41. Ibid., 222.

42. Ellis Cose, "The Myth of Meritocracy," *Newsweek*, April 3, 1995, 34.

43. Mark G. Kelman, "Concepts of Discrimination in 'General Ability' Job Testing," *Harvard Law Review* 104 (1991): 1158.

44. This and other related arguments are presented in Hilton Kramer and Roger Kimball, eds., *The Survival of Culture: Permanent Values in a Virtual Age* (Chicago: Ivan R. Dee, 2002). The question is raised as to how the cultural values that have distinguished Western civilization can survive the present-day preoccupation with relativism. Also raised is the issue of how Western values can be defended against the anti-Western forces that operate within the West itself.

45. Mona Charen, "Fueling the Campus Cauldron," *Washington Times*, March 28, 2005.

46. Kimball, "Institutionalizing Our Demise."

47. Jim Rutenberg, "Poll Question Stirs Debate on Meaning of 'Values,'" *New York Times*, November 6, 2004.

48. Bruce Bawer, "Tolerant Dutch Wrestle with Tolerating Intolerance," *New York Times*, November 14, 2004.

49. Editorial, "Dutch Counterterrorism," *Washington Times*, November 15, 2004.

50. Francis Fukuyama, "A Year of Living Dangerously," *Wall Street Journal*, November 2, 2005.

51. Tony Blankley, "Europe to the Barricades," *Washington Times*, November 24, 2004.

52. Charles Krauthammer, "What the Uprising Generation Wants," *Time*, November 21, 2005, 162.

53. Kimball, "Institutionalizing Our Demise."

54. Ibid.

55. Leo McKinstry, "Dis-United Kingdom," *Weekly Standard*, December 5, 2005, 12.

56. Ibid., 14.

57. Heather MacDonald, "Get Serious About Immigration Enforcement," *Dallas Morning News*, December 30, 2004.

58. Ibid.

Chapter 8: THE SHACKLES OF GUILT

1. Brian C. Anderson, "Secular Europe, Religious America," *Public Interest* (Spring 2004): 143.

2. Niall Ferguson, "The Widening Atlantic," *Atlantic Monthly*, January–February 2005, 44.

3. Anderson, "Secular Europe, Religious America."

4. Ferguson, "The Widening Atlantic," 44

5. Anderson, "Secular Europe, Religious America."

6. Tessa Keswick, quoted in Helle Dale, "Bridging the Allies' Divide," WashingtonTimes.com, November 24, 2004.

7. Ibid.

8. David Pryce-Jones, "Mass-Hysteria Time," *National Review*, November 29, 2004, 30. In *Vile France: Fear, Duplicity, Cowardice and Cheese*, Dennis Boyles describes a France that let fifteen thousand of its elderly die in the heat wave of August 2003 as their relatives refused to cut short their summer vacations, and that readily exercises unilateral power when it wishes (as in Ivory Coast) while condemning it elsewhere. The moral emptiness of contemporary German culture is reflected in the story of an unemployed Berlin waitress who faced loss of welfare benefits after refusing a job as a prostitute in a legal brothel. Mark Steyn, "Tolerance Fetish," *Washington Times*, February 14, 2005.

9. Ferguson, "The Widening Atlantic," 40.

10. HR 40, 109th Cong., 1st sess. (2005).

11. In 2003, twenty-two representatives cosponsored the bill. Despite the unprecedented nature of the reparations movement, it has attracted the support of people like Alan Keyes, a former Republican candidate for president who has reversed his longtime opposition to reparations. Although he once referred to reparations as "an insult to our slave ancestors," Keyes now supports a plan that would exempt the descendants of slaves from income taxes for at least a generation. Christine Phillip, "Reversal of Attitude," MSNBC.com, www.msnbc.msn.com/id /5747800/print/1/displaymode/1098.

12. J. A. Parker, *Huntsville Chronicle*, www.thehunstvillechronicle.com/articles /Chicago/reparation.htm.

13. www.freep.com/news/politics/gov4–20021004.htm.

14. "CDI Releases Slavery Era Insurance Survey," *Insurance Journal*, May 2, 2002, http://www.insurancejournal.com/news/west/2002/05/02/17531.htm.

15. "City Contractors Must Reveal Slavery Ties," United Press International, October 3, 2002.

16. Joyce Howard Price, "Detroit Joins 2 Cities on Slave Disclosures," *Washington Times*, July 1, 2004, http://www.washingtontimes.com/national/20040701–122147 –7163r.htm.

17. Conrad Worrill, "The Tactic of Lawsuits and the Reparations Movement," *Jackson (MS) Advocate*, January 8, 2004.

18. Peter Flaherty and John Carlisle, *The Case Against Slave Reparations* (Falls Church, VA: National Legal and Policy Center, 2004), 13.

19. Ibid., 15.

20. Herbert S. Klein, *The Atlantic Slave Trade* (New York: Cambridge University Press, 1999), 99, 58, 106–7, 155, 159.

21. Flaherty and Carlisle, *Case Against Slave Reparations*, 23.

22. Walter Williams, Creators Syndicate/Washington Times, November 24, 2002.

23. "Boston Police Must End Affirmative Action Hiring, U.S. Judge Says," *Minneapolis Star Tribune*, November 25, 2004.

24. Institutions of higher education, for instance, maintain a complex labyrinth of racial preferences, many of which are illegal. David J. Armor, "Affirmative Action at Three Universities," paper presented at the Virginia Association of Scholars Annual Meeting, November 13, 2004.

25. In *Coloring the News*, William McGowan demonstrates how police departments in various cities have experienced corruption, incompetence, and lawlessness from hiring officers whose applications have been rushed through in a sprint to boost minority employment. William McGowan, *Coloring the News: How Crusading for Diversity Has Corrupted American Journalism* (San Francisco: Encounter Books, 2001), 151, 154–55.

26. Don Scoggins, quoted in Heather MacDonald, "Heralds of a Brighter Black Future," *City Journal*, Spring 2005.

27. John McWhorter, "Who Should Get into College?" *City Journal*, Spring 2003, www.city-journal.org/html/13_2_who_should_get.html.

28. Richard Sander, "A Systemic Analysis of Affirmative Action in American Law Schools," *Stanford Law Review* 57 (2004): 367, 371.

29. Ibid.

30. Ibid., 372.

31. Ibid., 454.

32. Ibid., 482.

33. McWhorter, "Who Should Get into College?"

34. Ibid.

35. Ibid.

36. McWhorter, "Who Should Get into College?"

37. Larry Elder, "Chicken-ism Mission," *Washington Times*, February 13, 2005, www.washingtontimes.com/functions/print.php?storyID=20050212–093433 –7134r.

38. Rachel F. Moran, "Diversity and Its Discontents: The End of Affirmative Action at Boalt Hall," *California Law Review* 88 (2000): 2241, 2266.

39. As Jayson Blair, the black *New York Times* reporter fired for plagiarism, notes in his biography, *Burning Down My Masters' House*: "I knew by then that I had become some pawn in a racial game, and that my work mattered less than the politi-

cal points my success or failure gave to [the diversity concerns of the newspaper]" ([Beverly Hills, CA: New Millennium, 2004], 151).

40. Peter Brimelow and Leslie Spencer, "When Quotas Replace Merit, Everybody Suffers," *Forbes*, February 15, 1993, 102. The budgets of just the federal government agencies charged with monitoring racial discrimination accusations reach into the hundreds of millions of dollars (Dinesh D'Souza, *The End of Racism: Principles for a Multiracial Society* [New York: Free Press, 1995], 320).

41. Jay Nordlinger, "Color in Coaching," *National Review*, September 1, 2003, 25.

42. Ibid.

43. Ellis Cose, "Does Cosby Help?" *Newsweek*, December 27, 2004, 66.

44. Ibid.

45. James Taranto, "What's Behind Liberal Racism," WSJ.com Opinion Journal, December 10, 2004.

Conclusion

1. Joseph S. Nye, "Introduction: The Decline of Confidence in Government," in *Why People Don't Trust Government*, ed. Joseph S. Nye Jr., Philip D. Zelikow, and David C. King (Cambridge, MA: Harvard University Press, 1997). 1.

2. Ibid.

3. Eric Schmitt, "Citing Terrorism Threat, Pentagon Will Close Its Child Care Center; Many Are Outraged," *New York Times*, July 15, 2004.

IndEx